SCENTED TREASURES

SCENTED TREASURES

Aromatic Gifts from Kitchen & Garden

STEPHANIE DONALDSON

PHOTOGRAPHY BY SHONA WOOD

A Storey Publishing Book

Storey Communications, Inc.
Schoolhouse Road
Pownal, Vermont 05261

To the four 'J's' in my life

United States edition published in 1996 by
Storey Communications, Inc., Schoolhouse Road,
Pownal, Vermont 05261

First published in the UK in 1995 by
New Holland (Publishers) Ltd
24 Nutford Place, London W1H 6DQ

ISBN 0 88266 930 3

Editorial direction Yvonne McFarlane
Editor Coral Walker
Art director Jane Forster
Photographer Shona Wood
Illustrator Claire Davies
Cover photograph of author John Freeman
Storey Communications editor Gwen Steege

Phototypeset by Ace Filmsetting Ltd, Frome, Somerset
Printed and bound in Singapore by Tien Wah Press (Pte.) Ltd.

Important: In the recipes, use either metric or imperial measurements,
but not a combination of the two, as exact conversions are not always
possible. Every effort has been made to present clear and accurate
instructions. Therefore, the author and publishers can accept no
liability for any injury, illness or damage which may inadvertently be
caused to the user while following these instructions. The essential oils
used in aromatherapy have very powerful properties. In this book, we
explain some of them; for specific treatment, it is vital that you consult
a recognized aromatherapist.

Author's Acknowledgements

First of all, grateful thanks to Jane, Shona and Coral
for their superhuman efforts, which were noticed
and much appreciated.

In addition, the author and publishers would like to
thank the following people and companies for their
help.

Touch Design Ltd, P.O. Box 60, Andover SP11 6SS
(Tel: 01264 738060) for the various planters, trays,
vases and candleholders.

The wine department at Selfridges, Oxford Street,
London W1, for the loan of the presentation box for
wine on page 119.

Hertford Antiques, 51 St Andrews Street, Hertford
SG14 1H2 (Tel: 01920 460468) for the antique glass
on pages 25, 69 and 125.

Louise Pope, Rheidol House, Devil's Bridge,
Aberystwyth SY23 4QY (Tel: 01970 890288)
for the cupboard on page 51.

Graham Carter, 16 Mehetebel Road, London E8 6DU
(Tel: 0181-985-4494) for the cupboards on pages 41,
91, and the chest on page 121.

Tsar Architectural, 487 Liverpool Road, London N7
8PG (Tel: 0171 609 4238) for the tiles on page 85.

Fleur Aromatherapy and Neal's Yard Remedies for
the box and bottles on page 97.

Simon Rich, Narbeth Pottery, Narbeth, Dyfed SA67
7AX (Tel: 01834 860732) for the dish on page 55.

Library of Congress Cataloging-in-Publication Data

Donaldson, Stephanie.
Scented treasures: aromatic gifts from your kitchen
and garden/Stephanie Donaldson.
p. cm.
Includes bibliographical references and index.
ISBN 0 88266 930 3 (hardcover: alk. paper)
1. Nature craft. 2. Herbs–Utilization. 3. Cookery
(Herbs). 4. Potpourris (Scented floral mixtures)
5. Herbal cosmetics. 6. Essences and essential oils.
7. Spices. I. Title
TT157.D628   1996   96-10642
745.5–dc20   CIP

Contents

INTRODUCTION 8

SPRING

13

SUMMER

43

AUTUMN

71

WINTER

99

BIBLIOGRAPHY 126

INDEX 128

Foreword

As a child I was much taken with making "concoctions," most of which succeeded in transforming base matter into something quite dreadful; among the most memorable being the "perfume" I made by mixing 'California Poppy' with gripe water (see page 28)! I shall not be revealing the secret of that particular blend in this book, but I do hope that I shall inspire you to share my enjoyment of aromatics.

I am fascinated by the effect that scent has upon our lives, its ability to alter mood, to conjure up the past, a place or a person, with astonishing clarity. Smell is a feeling, not a thought; the wonderful smell of a tiny baby's neck sends me hurtling back to when my children were babies, a Fragonard fragrance conjures up memories of a tempestuous love affair, the gooseberry scent of Sancerre recalls the first time I tasted the wine in the French hilltop town and, even blindfolded, I would recognize home by the unique blend of aromas that greet me when I open my front door.

The dictionary definition of aromatic is, "Fragrant, spicy, pleasantly pungent." It is a definition which encompasses all aspects of fragrance, from the sophistication of fine perfume, through the heady scents of the flower garden to the delicious aromas of the kitchen. At its simplest, it is a bunch of flowers or a twist of lemon and at its most complex, it is a blend of essential oils gained from the distillation of thousands of hand-picked flowers.

There has always been magic and mystery associated with aromatics, their exotic origins and their powerful effects. Many myths and legends have grown up around aromatics, religions have used them to enhance ceremonies, and they are an essential ingredient in most festivals. I share this respect for their powers, using them regularly for health and relaxation, to influence mood, create atmosphere and flavor foods, always taking sybaritic pleasure in their powers to enrich my life.

In this book, I follow aromatics through the seasons: the fresh, green, citrus scents of spring, the warm, voluptuous, heady fragrance of summer, the pungent, woody, fruity aromas of autumn, and the rich, spicy, resinous fragrances of winter. All are explored with appropriate seasonal projects. Although the central theme of the book is aromatic gifts, one of the great virtues of working with fragrances is that they offer pleasure to the giver as well as the recipient, and like myself, you may soon find yourself working on a 'one for them, one for me' basis, as you find yourself reluctant to part with the fruits of your labors.

Scented Treasures includes inspirational ideas for scented plants for the garden, clever concepts for presenting flowers and herbs, recipes that reflect the seasonal flavors, and lotions and potions for health and beauty. Each season also has its own potpourri and aromatics for the linen closet, bedroom and bathroom.

It has been my intention, in writing this book, to convey something of my enthusiasm and appreciation of aromatics and to inspire you to begin to explore this endlessly fascinating subject. Before you turn the pages, it is illuminating, exhilarating and sometimes amusing to look at the history of aromatics and the influence of smell in our lives.

Introduction

The history of aromatics is the history of the civilized world. For thousands of years, wherever aromatics have been valued for their fragrance, their healing powers, their calming, stimulant, and aphrodisiac qualities, it is evidence of a society which has risen above mere survival.

The earliest form of perfume was incense, the word perfume is derived from the Latin *perfumum* meaning "through smoke." Oils scented with herbs were used for anointing and cleansing the body as long ago as 1000 years BC.

Egyptians were the first to make use of scented oils in their baths. These were followed by massage with aromatic oils. Cosmetics were also an important part of Egyptian life: mascara was used to shade the eyes from the sun and one Egyptian recipe promised to turn an old man into a youth, while another claimed to expel wrinkles. It was the Egyptians who first recorded using the process of *enfleurage*, where animal fats are used to absorb

the fragrance from flowers. Egypt is still one of the world's greatest producers of essential oil plants.

From the 7th century BC, the Greeks traded their goods for the materials to make fragrant oils using lilies, marjoram, thyme, sage, roses, anise and iris root. Alexander the Great brought Persian civilization to Greece, and from his travels he sent back seeds and cuttings to Theophrastus who established the first botanic garden and wrote *Concerning Odours*, a treatise on scent.

By the time of Christ, true frankincense and myrrh were in use, as well as gum galbanum, which is now used in "green" note perfumes such as Vent Vert.

The Ancient Romans – both male and female – perfumed themselves liberally and even scented their pets and horses, while the Persians learned how to extract oils from flowers by distillation and became expert perfume makers.

India has the richest diversity of aromatic plants in the world. Traditionally, its people are scrupulously clean and fragrant oils, pastes and powders have long been part of the bathing ritual. As well as fragrancing their bodies they used aromatics in their buildings. Sandalwood was used for the important entrances of temples, which were also known as houses of fragrance. Vetiver roots were used to make screens which when dampened gave off an odor reminiscent of violets.

The Chinese and Japanese have always scented the environment rather than the body. There is a possible physiological reason for this as the apocrine glands which create body odor are virtually

Roses continue to flower right into the middle of winter (below left). This rosebud's fragile beauty is further enhanced by the delicate outline of frost crystals. An unmistakeable medley of autumn colors (right): the golden, russet and ruby hues of mixed flowers, fruits and foliage of the season.

non-existent in South-East Asians. Additionally, the bath has always been very important in these cultures while there have been frequent taboos on bathing in the west. The oriental nations believe that use of fragrance helps to prolong life. The gimbel or perfume burner has been present in Chinese houses for well over 2000 years.

In Europe, "modern" perfume did not appear until 1370, when it was formulated as Hungary Water. Named after Queen Elizabeth of Hungary, it was based on oil of rosemary with lavender added. This was followed by Eau de Carmes – a blend of lemon balm and angelica made by the Carmelite nuns of St Juste. Lavender water was next to appear and this was recommended for internal as well as external use.

The main function of early perfumes was to freshen the outside of the body – this was much needed, as bathing was considered dangerous to the body and the soul.

The arrival of the plague created a great demand for herbs and spices. Cities were "purified" by the burning of spices in the squares. Essential oils are in fact powerful germicides, but in the small quantities that were used they were no match for the filth of medieval cities, although later on it was observed that the perfumery workers of Grasse suffered less from tuberculosis and cholera than the rest of the population of Europe.

With the coming of the Renaissance, Venice quickly established itself as a leader in aromatics. Unfortunately, the trade of the city was seriously affected when Constantinople fell to the Ottoman Turks, which severed the spice routes between Europe and Asia. Explorers of the day sought alternative routes, and in 1498 the Portuguese explorer Vasco da Gama completed the route round Africa to India and returned to Lisbon with a fortune in spices. This had a further disastrous effect on Venice and the Venetians plotted with the Egyptians in an attempt to re-establish their pre-eminence as the trading center of spices and aromatics in Europe. They engaged in battle with the Portuguese and a final decisive battle left the Portuguese victorious. The center of trade shifted from the Mediterranean to the Atlantic.

Control of the Spice Trade moved between European nations as they attempted to monopolize the East. The Dutch gained supremacy with the Dutch East India Company and the British and French also gained important footholds. Even today the association of South-East Asian countries with their former colonial powers can be traced back to the Western thirst for spices.

It was not until the Rococo period that perfume production reached near industrial scale under the influence of Madame de Pompadour and Marie Antoinette. Scented vinegars were used to tone the skin after bathing. It became fashionable to receive guests while bathing with a cover over the bath for modesty. Scented fans were used for flirtation and scented pomades in beautiful porcelain containers became popular. Potpourri was in general use. Scented hair powder and make-up were essential and perfumed clothes were kept in aromatic clothes presses.

The early blooms are sometimes the most precious: snowdrops combine with helebores and winter foliage in a simple, yet enchanting posy.

However, the greatest scent of the age was not French. An Italian barber who went to Germany first marketed his "water" Eau de Cologne in 1709. Around the same time in England a Spaniard named Juan Floris set up a business in London selling scented powders, scents and pots pourris. Thomas Yardley was granted a charter in 1770 and in 1780 he began producing his famous Lavender Water, now synonymous with scent.

At the end of the 18th century, the French Revolution sent the perfume industry into decline for 50 years. With the advent of Napoleon a new era began. He created a new nobility of talent and financed scientific research. He was also fastidiously clean and often used several bottles of Eau de Cologne a day. The recipe for Eau de Cologne was much copied and many legal actions resulted.

The rights were eventually bought by Roger & Gallet in 1862.

The 19th century saw the birth of the modern perfume industry. At the Paris International Exhibition in 1867, perfumery occupied a whole section. Ladies of the time made extensive use of aromatics: flower waters were used liberally, patent medicines were consumed in vast quantities, houses and conservatories were filled with fragrant flowers and in the kitchen the effect of British colonial expansion meant that exotic spices were freely available and used in new and adventurous ways.

The 1920s was the decade of Chanel, Patou, Molyneux and Lanvin. Chanel No. 5 was the first perfume to make use of an aldehyde (oxidized alcohol) and remains as popular today as it was 70 years ago. Joy, from Jean Patou, still symbolizes the height of luxury with its formulation that incorporates Bulgarian rose and jasmine absolute.

The term aromatherapy first appeared in the 1930s, but it is really only in the last 10 years that the therapeutic use of essential oils has become widespread as people turn to natural remedies as an adjunct to conventional medicine.

During the first half of the 20th century the culinary use of aromatic herbs and spices was fairly unadventurous and the Second World War meant that anything that was not home-grown was nearly impossible to obtain. All this changed dramatically during the post-war years with the explosion in foreign travel which introduced everyone to new tastes and flavors.

spring

When the honeyed wine of
  apple blossom is in the air
    and the freshness of the dew is
  like a caress, we hear the youth
of the world laughing –
  we see Perdita with her arms full of
  daffodils,
  and Atalanta coming through
    the meadows with wet, white feet.

THE JOY OF FRAGRANCE
  Mary Webb (1881–1927)

Suddenly, it seems that previously cozy rooms have become stuffy, and I know it's time to fling windows open and let in the fresh scents of spring. In the garden, all that was static is now in motion, and the smell of growth is everywhere. There is so much to do, but there must also be time to stop and smell the flowers, for, as the days warm up, the strength of the sun quickly transforms those delicate first scents of spring into something more heady and robust, and I do not want to miss any of it.

In the kitchen, it's time to throw out the remains of the dried herbs and enjoy freshly picked chives and mint, rosemary veiled in blue flowers and the first sprigs of tarragon. The tang of lemons fills the air as they are peeled, grated and squeezed for use in recipes to enhance taste and add piquancy to spring dishes.

Vases of fresh flowers and pots of bulbs bring the new season indoors and I make bowls of citrus potpourri to replace the spicy winter mix that went before, dramatically changing the mood of the house, which is now light, bright and airy where previously it was warmly cloistered.

Aromatic spring gifts are always well received and making them need not be an elaborate or expensive process: a simple bouquet of freshly picked herbs tied with garden string, a bowl of fragrant bulbs nestling in moss, or a jar of pickled lemons are all gifts with a personal touch.

There is now a delicious, light sharpness to the scents in the garden – in the language of parfumiers, these are said to have predominantly "green" notes.

What wonderful moments they are – those bright, new days in spring, when the pale primroses and deep violets release their soft scent in the warm sun; when the woods are carpeted with balsam-scented bluebells and the first of the season's fresh green herbs are waiting to be picked. The air is full of sharp, green, citrus scents and you long to be out in the open air, enjoying every single minute of those very special days.

The warmth of the sun is not always guaranteed early in the season and the fragrance of the flowers cuts through crisp, cool air, attracting the attention of pollinating insects.

Certain flowers are a must for planting in the aromatic spring garden. Jonquils, narcissus, grape hyacinths, primroses and polyanthus all create a symphony of scents and color of exquisite freshness. At the tail end of autumn, it's hard to feel much enthusiasm for gardening, but I always try to plant some wallflowers – and now those dull green bundles which I firmed into the soil so long ago have turned into gloriously scented flowers.

If you have a cool, shady corner in the garden, it is worth establishing a lily of the valley bed. For best results, dig in plenty of leaf-mold, peat or peat substitute, so that the soil is moisture-retentive, rich and free-draining. The plants will take a couple of years to get established, but once they are, they will spread rapidly and you will be able to pick clusters of these fragrant flowers.

Shrubs have their greatest glory in the spring and you should try to find room for some of the most aromatic. Oregon grape *(Mahonia aquifolium)* is deliciously fragrant and has the added advantage that it will grow practically anywhere; it doesn't mind dry shade or impoverished soil and will reward you with yellow flowers whose honey scent is among the strongest fragrances in the early spring garden. The white, spring-flowering viburnums are also desirable. *V.* × *burkwoodii* has the advantage of being evergreen, but *V.* × *carlesii* and *V.* × *juddii* are also highly recommended. Try to find a sunny corner for *Daphne × burkwoodii* 'Somerset', and position a seat next to it, so that on sunny days you can drink in its glorious scent. If you also have plantings of lilac and the *Rhododendron luteum*, you can experience olfactory bliss!

One spring, I went to the late Vita Sackville-West's wonderful garden, Sissinghurst in the south of England. I sat in the white garden admiring the beauty of all that surrounded me and noticed, over my head, a stunningly beautiful, scented, white wisteria in full bloom. I was so impressed that, having noted its name, *Wisteria venusta*, I later ordered one from a specialist nursery for my own garden. It has yet to flower, but one day I shall be able to sit in my garden and recall that perfect moment at Sissinghurst. All wisterias have some smell, but it does vary, so for an aromatic garden, ensure you choose a variety that is noted for its scent.

If you are lucky enough to have a greenhouse, or you are living in a temperate climate, a mimosa tree is a richly aromatic reminder of a Mediterranean spring.

She to no state or dignity aspires,
But silent and alone puts on her suit,
And sheds a lasting perfume, but for which
We had not known there was a thing so sweet
Hid in the gloomy shade.

THE LILY OF THE VALLEY
James Hurdis (1763–1801)

LILY OF THE VALLEY (*Convallaria majalis*) prefers to hide in the shade, as James Hurdis's poem intimates. Because of this, its hauntingly beautiful scent can easily be missed. In the garden of my last house, these plants had established themselves in the middle of a shady hedge and to appreciate their scent and beauty it was necessary to get down on hands and knees and thrust one's head into the middle of the hedge!

In the Middle Ages, a distillation from lily of the valley called *aqua aurea* was considered to have great healing properties and was so highly valued that it was kept in specially made gold and silver receptacles. In a 1657 *Herbal*, directions for its preparation went as follows: "Take the flowers and steep them in New Wine for the space of a month; which being finished, take them out again and distil the wine three times over in a Limbeck. The wine is more precious than gold, for if anyone that is troubled with apoplexy drink thereof with six grains of Pepper and a little Lavender water they shall not need to fear it." As the lily of the valley contains a substance similar to digitalis, which is the active agent in the foxglove, it may well be that there was some beneficial effect in the *aqua aurea*.

A modern equivalent – which is a scent and not potable – can be made by filling a small bottle with lily of the valley flowers and topping it up with vodka. Strain and replace the flowers weekly for as long as the flowers last. At the end of the process, you will have a lily of the valley-scented cologne. This would make a charming gift, especially if it is decanted into an antique scent bottle.

Lily of the valley pots

Lily of the valley will grow well in pots and, if planted in autumn and kept in a cool greenhouse or cold frame over winter, they will be ready to be brought indoors to flower in early spring. The plants grow from creeping, horizontal rhizomes and can be bought bare-root as "pips" in the autumn or in pots at any time of year. The pip is the little, pointed, embryo leaf spike which indicates where the plant will sprout.

To package as a gift, line a pretty wirework basket with sphagnum moss, rest a plastic saucer on the base of the basket and nestle the plants in the center. Tie a gift tag to the basket and write out care instructions.

24 lily of the valley pips

Eight 3 in (7 cm) square plastic pots

Potting mix made up of:
3 parts loam, 3 parts leaf-mold, 1 part sharp sand

Two 6 in (15 cm) decorative pots or a rectangular container approximately 10 × 8 in (25 × 20 cm)

Sphagnum moss

Gift packaging materials, optional

Pot three pips to each pot, so that the pips are just below the surface of the potting mixture. Firm in gently. Water and place in a cool greenhouse or cold frame for the winter. Only water if the plants dry out.

The plants will start into growth in the late winter or early spring and can be brought indoors or into a heated greenhouse. Frequent watering will be necessary for rapid growth. Just before they flower they can be repotted into the decorative pots, or placed in their pots in a plastic-lined basket and surrounded by moss.

The fragile beauty and sweet scent of the lily of the valley can really be appreciated when they are planted in a decorative container.

SPRING FLOWERS really announce the arrival of this most welcome season. Personally, one of the defining moments of spring is the day when there are sufficient flowers in the garden for me to pick a bunch without feeling that I am detracting from the display. Earlier on, I may take the occasional scented sprig or single bloom to add to cut flowers, but the pleasure of that first home-gathered bouquet is incomparable.

One of the delights of French country markets is the sight of stallholders selling off surplus produce from their gardens – a basket of eggs, three jars of honey, some bundles of fragrant herbs and tiny scented posies of seasonal blooms. The first time I saw this was in the flower market at Tours, in central France. There were stalls of extravagant beauty with huge bundles of heady lilies and lilac, but tucked in among this opulence were stalls of great modesty where elderly women sold homemade posies that won my heart. The simple beauty of their posies lay in the fact that they had not been "designed," but were made up from the flowers that had been gathered from the garden. There was an informality seldom seen in florists' flowers.

Where one would hesitate to cut a branch from a precious scented shrub, a couple of sprigs can safely be spared to make the heart of a posy, and even in early spring you will be amazed at what you can find in the garden to complete the arrangement. It is always satisfying to give a really personal gift and these are always much appreciated by their recipients.

Spring posy

What you put in your posy obviously depends on what you have available; you may think that you have little that is scented in your garden, but the fact is most flowers have some scent, however subtle, and a posy is the best possible way to appreciate it. In very early spring, a posy of delicate white snowdrops surrounded by ivy leaves has a touching beauty and a delicate fragrance. Grape hyacinths, bellis daisies and forget-me-nots look wonderful tied with a bright bow, while jonquils, small yellow tulips and golden sage makes an eye-catching and aromatic combination.

A selection of spring flowers from the garden
Garden twine
Ribbon

To form the center of the posy hold a bunch of one type of flower in your hand. Add a row of contrasting flowers around the central group until it is completely surrounded. Continue adding rows of contrasting flowers until the posy has reached the required size. Add a row of overlapping leaves.

Bind the posy with twine. Trim the stems and cover the twine with a decorative ribbon.

Mix flowers and foliage from the garden with some bought blooms as I have done with this pretty grouping. Bellis daisies and grape hyacinths picked from the garden are surrounded with florists' jonquils and finished with early euphorbia, brunnera and aquilegia leaves to create a fragrant posy.

VIOLETS *(Viola odorata)* – of all the aromatic plants – are some of the most mysterious, with their elusive scent which has enchanted poets and rulers alike. Shakespeare had more than a passing acquaintance with the flowers, as Stratford-upon-Avon was once as famous for its violets as it now is as the birthplace of the Bard.

Napoleon and Josephine both adored violets and she wore a violet scent as her trademark. When he spurned her, she exacted a scented revenge by having the Imperial Apartments drenched with heavy and persistent musk oil which he loathed. It must have worn off eventually because upon her death he had her grave carpeted with violets and wore a locket of the flowers picked from the grave until his own death.

Josephine's successor, Marie-Louise, also loved violets, and when she, too, was rejected she retired to Parma, where she established production of the Parma violet and the making of violet water. When Napoleon went to Elba, his final message to his followers was that he should return with violets. From then on he was secretly toasted by them as Caporal Violette and the pretty, purple flower became the emblem of the Imperial Napoleonic party.

The elusiveness of the violet scent has a chemical explanation. It contains ionone, which short-circuits our sense of smell. When smelling the flower, its scent quickly fades, but if you leave the flower and return to it after a few minutes – the scent will be there once more, only to fade yet again! It plays hide and seek with our olfactory nerves, making it impossible to get too much of it. This is not true of synthetic violet which is universally used in fragrances. Sadly, these days, the harvesting of violet flowers and the extraction of their scent is a far too expensive process, although the leaves are used to provide a green note in some commercial fragrances.

There is a long tradition of using violets in food and for medicinal purposes. Homer, Virgil and Pliny all refer to its power to "lessen anger and strengthen the heart" and Pliny describes how a garland of violets worn on the brow will moderate the effects of alcohol. Until quite recently, syrup of violets was a popular medicine for its gently laxative effect and in earlier times it was considered one of the great cure-alls.

John Gerard, the 17th-century English herbalist said, "It has power to ease inflammation,

roughness of the throat and comforteth the heart, assuageth the pains of the head and causeth sleep." Additionally, violet leaves were a popular folk remedy, being used to make healing poultices and to relieve bruising.

The use of violets in cooking has always been mainly decorative, and in France, using flowers in salads and to decorate cakes is a long-established practice. Crystallized violets and violet sugars have been popular culinary items for many hundreds of years.

Frosted violets

Just above Nice, in the south of France, is a village called Tourrette-sur-Loup, which is known locally as the Cité de Violette. In the past, it was the center of the violet-growing area that served the nearby perfume industry of Grasse. Sadly today, this is all in the past, although the tourist shops still do a brisk trade in crystallized violets of a purple so lurid that one fears for one's safety when eating them!

Crystallizing flowers is a fiddly and time-consuming process, but provided that you are planning to use the flowers within 24 hours, frosting is an easier alternative. Frosted violets can be used to decorate cakes or as pretty toppings for ice creams and puddings. They can be stored in an airtight container, but are at their best used immediately before their scent has had time to evaporate.

Violets
1 lightly whisked egg white
Soft paintbrush
Castor sugar
Wire rack covered with baking parchment

Gently paint the petals of the flowers on both sides with egg white. Dust the flowers thoroughly with the castor sugar. Gently shake to remove excess sugar. Place the frosted flowers on the parchment-covered rack and leave in a warm place to dry for about 2 hours.

Sometimes the simplest finishing touches are the best: unfussy, uncluttered and not contrived. Frosted flowers fit into this category as nature has done all the hard work and my part is simple. These violets make beautiful decorations for a plain iced cake.

Violet salad

The aromatic element of this recipe comes not from the elusive violet fragrance but from the dressing made with walnut oil and raspberry vinegar which creates flavors as intense as the colors of this delicious salad. The salad is delicious on its own or served with cured meats such as Parma ham or bresaola.

For a pretty gift, make up a jar of the dressing and place it in a decorative basket lined with a purple table napkin. Add a bunch of violets or a potted violet plant together with a card giving the salad recipe.

FOR THE WALNUT OIL DRESSING
1 tsp Dijon mustard
Crushed clove of garlic
Juice of 1 lemon
2 tbsp raspberry vinegar
1 tsp sugar
Salt and pepper to taste
½ cup (100 ml) walnut oil
½ cup (100 ml) peanut oil

FOR THE SALAD
2 'Little Gem' lettuces
2 bunches of trimmed watercress
Head of blanched chicory or frisée
Bunch of dark purple violets
Wide glass salad bowl
Gift packaging, optional
Serves 6

The forward violet thus did I chide;
Sweet thief, whence didst thou steal
thy sweet that smells,
If not from my love's breath?

SONNET XCIX
William Shakespeare (1564–1616)

First, make up the dressing. Place all the ingredients except the oils in a blender and blend thoroughly. With the motor running, slowly pour the oils into the mixture and continue to blend until you have a smooth, creamy-looking dressing.

Thoroughly wash and drain the lettuces, watercress and chicory or frisée. Wash the violets carefully (this is particularly important if they are bought rather than home-grown). Gently shake dry. Pinch off the stem and calyx from each flower – you will only use the petals. Place all the salad ingredients except the violet flowers in the bowl and pour on the salad dressing. Toss well. Sprinkle the violet flowers over the salad and serve immediately.

To store any leftover dressing, pour into a jar and keep in the refrigerator. Stand at room temperature for half an hour before using.

The rich purple of the violets creates a beautiful contrast to the pale frisée, the blanched chicory and the deeper greens of the cos lettuce and the watercress.

ELDER (Sambucus nigra), with its abundant, foaming white flowers, gives the hedgerows an air of celebration. Although the plant itself has a rather rank smell, elderflowers are used to make a deliciously muscat-scented cordial. Elderflowers have been used for centuries to make healing ointments and salves and elderflower water is a gently astringent skin tonic.

In traditional folklore the elder is considered to be the "Mother Herb" and no one should cut any part of it without first asking the tree's permission. Throughout Europe, the plant was much respected: the Russians planted it to drive away evil spirits, Sicilians used its wood as protection against serpents, and at traditional Serb wedding ceremonies a twig of elder was included for good luck.

$\mathcal{S}pring\ cordial$

This delicious, refreshing drink made from elderflowers has a long country tradition. Serve as a refreshing drink diluted with four parts of sparkling mineral water, or use as a flavoring for a sorbet or in place of cassis in a kir royale. It can be drunk immediately but will keep indefinitely.

6 cups (1.5 kg) granulated sugar
6 cups (1.5 litre) boiling water
Large bowl or non-metallic bucket
¼ cup (50 g) citric acid
25 elderflowerheads, washed and shaken dry
2 washed and sliced lemons
Strainer and muslin
Decorative bottles and labels, optional
Makes 2½ quarts of concentrated cordial

Dissolve the sugar in the boiling water, pour into a container and leave to cool. Stir in the citric acid. Add the elderflower heads and sliced lemons. Stir and cover with a cloth. Infuse for 2 days, stirring occasionally. Strain through muslin and pour into clean bottles with stoppers or screw tops. Store in a cool place as a little fermentation may take place.

This delicious elderflower cordial (above) is extremely versatile, a refreshing drink, a delicate addition to kirs and champagne, and an unusual complement to fruit salads. Alternatively, use elderflowers to make this stimulating skin tonic (far right).

Elderflower skin tonic

Elderflower water makes a light and very pleasing skin tonic. If you are picking the flowers for this tonic in deepest countryside, it probably isn't necessary to wash them, but if you are foraging near to a busy road, rinse the flowerheads under a cold tap. Store full bottles of the tonic in the refrigerator and, once open, keep in a cool place away from bright light. It's advisable to use within one month.

To package for a friend, photocopy an old botanical illustration of an elderflower, cut it out and hand-color as a decorative label for a presentation bottle of elderflower water. Attach a gift tag with instructions on use and storage.

50 elderflower heads
Sterilized glass jar of 1 quart (1 litre) capacity
2½ cups (600 ml) boiling water
5 tbsp (75 ml) vodka
Muslin for straining
Sterilized decorative glass bottles
Gift packaging, optional
Makes 3 cups (750 ml)

Gently strip the elderflowers from the flowerheads; stalks must not be used. Pack the flowers into the glass jar. Pour on the boiling water and leave to stand for half an hour. Add the vodka, cover and leave to stand in a warm place overnight. The following day, strain the elderflower water through muslin, decant into the glass bottles and seal.

. . . What gardeners they were:
what arbours of trellis work: embroidered
intricacies of bright nosegay-knots;
thrift and lavender
scented walks of evergreen;
what salves and syrops
of simple herbs for health and provender

GARDENS
Neil Curry (1937–)

The warm orange and yellow of pot marigolds make a delightful addition to any spring garden (right). Pot up a few to take to a garden-loving friend. If your friends are enthusiastic cooks, tie a bunch of fresh herbs with ribbon or twine as a simple but most welcome gift (far right).

POT MARIGOLDS or CALENDULAS (*Calendula officinalis*) were, in the past, an important culinary and medicinal herb grown universally in kitchen gardens and used for every imaginable purpose, from the culinary coloring of cheeses, and providing "petal pepper" for broths and stews (it still is in some countries, including Spain and North Africa), to the medicinal drawing out of evil humors, calming the heart and strengthening the eyesight.

Today, calendulas are chiefly grown as cheerful, easy and reliable cottage garden flowers which will self-seed everywhere, given the opportunity. The sturdy, aromatic flowers are ideal for picking and last well in water.

If space is limited, it is worthwhile growing one of the compact varieties of calendula in a pot so that you can use its bright petals to add color to a potato and chive salad. One and a half tablespoons of chopped fresh petals will make an unusual and flavorsome addition to a bread and butter pudding, while two tablespoons of dried petals can be added to one pound of rice instead of saffron. Or, take a leaf out of the old cookbooks and add a handful of dried petals to soups to impart savor and golden coloring.

To dry your own calendula petals for use as a pot herb or a potpourri ingredient, you should pick the flowers on a sunny morning after the dew has evaporated. Pull the petals from the flowerheads and spread them out loosely on paper. Place them in warm shade to dry quickly. Once dry, they can be stored in glass jars or brown paper bags.

The calendula is still a valued homeopathic remedy, with calendula ointment and cream widely used to promote healing of cuts and scratches.

FRESH HERBS are available now all the year round in the supermarkets, but it is still a delight to find a garden with some corner devoted to growing herbs. Since the beginning of recorded history much has been written about the health-giving, culinary and magical qualities of these plants and it would seem that we still need to nurture this instinctive association. Instead of taking a bunch of flowers to a friend, take a bouquet of fresh spring herbs.

Therewith her Vervain and her Dill,
That hindreth Witches of their Will

NYMPHIDIA
Michael Drayton (1563–1631)

DILL (Anethum graveolens) – a pretty annual herb – is a native of the Mediterranean, and its ability to soothe the digestion was known in ancient times when, according to Dioscorides, it was also used as a remedy against hiccups. In the Middle Ages, it was employed by magicians in their spells against witches. Aside from this rather esoteric use, the seeds of dill and fennel were eaten to alleviate hunger pangs, and pilgrims and travelers would carry a small bundle of the seeds to nibble as they walked. In Puritan times, it was considered acceptable to take some of the seeds to church to keep the attention from flagging.

An old-fashioned over-the-counter mixture called gripe water, the active ingredient of which is dill oil, was used as a universal remedy for infant colic and other digestive difficulties. It fell into disrepute because the formulation included alcohol and it was rightly felt that this would be harmful to babies. (It was additionally rumored that there were more than a few mothers who seemed to get through inordinate amounts of the patent medicine themselves!)

Dill is easily grown from seed, although it does prefer to be in the soil rather than in pots. As it is an attractive herb, I like to plant it in the flowerbed, rather than the vegetable garden, and its feathery aromatic foliage and yellow flowerheads look wonderful in a floral arrangement. Dill should not be planted near fennel as they tend to cross pollinate and the resultant seedlings are an unsatisfactory combination of the two plants.

In cooking, many dill recipes are Scandinavian in origin. For example, gravlax, the delicious salted salmon, is served with a sweet dill mustard sauce. The all-American hamburger would not be the same without dill pickles. Fresh dill is delicious chopped into a potato and mayonnaise salad and is a natural accompaniment to fish dishes.

CHIVES (Allium schoenoprasum) have been grown in gardens certainly since medieval times, although they were little written about and were clearly not thought to be of any great merit or importance. Culpeper took a dim view of the plant, for, in his *Complete Herbal*, he says, "I confess I had not added these had it not been for a country gentleman, who by a letter certified to me that amongst other herbs I had left these out. They are indeed a kind of leeks, hot and dry in the fourth degree . . . if they be eaten raw they send up very hurtful vapours to the brain, causing troublesome sleep and spoiling the eyesight."

Chives make a good edging to a path in the spring garden, although they tend to get straggly later in the year and should be cut regularly to prevent this happening. Alternatively, they can be planted just in front of a lavender hedge and by the time the chives are past their best, the lavender will have grown sufficiently to cover them.

While it is true that the chive is of no medicinal merit, it is a delicious culinary herb. Use chopped chives in salads, as a garnish for vegetables, in omelettes and with cream cheeses. This recipe for herb-coated goat cheeses uses freshly chopped chives as well as other spring herbs.

A man's nature runs either to herbs, or to weeds; therefore let him seasonably water the one and destroy the other.

Francis Bacon
(1561–1626)

Boules de chèvre
Goat cheese balls

Traditionally, goat cheese is at its best when the goats are first turned out after the winter and they browse on the fresh young shoots of spring. I have spent many happy holidays in the Sainte Maure region of France, the home of the finest goat cheeses, where cheeses of every description are produced, from the *chèvre doux*, a sweet soft cheese, to *crottins de Chavignol*, bullet-hard dry cheeses, so named because of their resemblance to the end product of the goat's digestive tract! Somewhere in the middle of these two extremes are the aromatic and flavorsome *boules*, which are balls of Montrachet or similar goat cheese formed into balls and gently rolled in herbs and spices. These *boules* couldn't be simpler to make at home, and provide a delicious accompaniment to pre-dinner drinks or an interesting addition to the cheese board.

For a portable gift, line a small basket or box with vine leaves or muslin, and take them to a friend as an alternative to a box of chocolates

6 oz (175 g) Montrachet or similar medium-firm goat cheese

6 natural-color drinking straws

A selection of finely chopped fresh herbs (chives, lemon thyme, mint, parsley, coriander, dill and rosemary are all suitable)

A selection of spices (cumin, paprika, black or pink peppercorns and celery seed)

Gift packaging, optional

Makes approximately 18 boules

Cut the cheese into small cubes roughly 1 in (2.5 cm) square. Roll each piece between your palms until they are circular. Cut the straw into pieces 3 in (7.5 cm) long and push one into the center of each *boule*. Holding the *boule* by the straw, gently roll it in the chopped herbs or spices until it is well covered.

Place on an uncovered plate in the refrigerator until needed. Arrange on a vine leaf-covered plate or straw mat to serve.

Goat cheese combines deliciously with chopped herbs and spices to make these colorful pre-dinner nibbles. The straw handles make them easy to manage even when you have a glass in your other hand.

PARSLEY (Petroselinum crispum) was considered by the Ancient Greeks to be one of their sacred herbs. Athletes were crowned with garlands of parsley, and because of its association with Persephone, tombs were decorated with wreaths made from it.

In the Middle Ages, it had the reputation of being able to destroy poison. This probably grew out of its ability to mask the strongest of odors (chew it raw to remove onion or garlic odors from the breath). Medicinally, it was commonly used as an effective diuretic. In French folk medicine, parsley and snails were pounded together, spread on a poultice and applied daily to cure glandular swellings. There is no comment on how efficacious this cure was, though personally I would rather have taken the snails by mouth with lashings of garlic and parsley butter!

In the garden, parsley is very slow to germinate and legend has it that this is because it descends seven times to hell before it starts to grow. It is also said that only an honest person can successfully grow parsley and that it should never be transplanted or it will bring bad luck. In spite of all of this, it is not a difficult herb to cultivate as long as you sow fresh seed. I like to grow curly parsley for use during the summer and the larger, hardier, flat-leaved parsley for use in winter.

In cooking, parsley is the herbal equivalent of the lemon with its ability to lift practically any dish to which it is added. To benefit fully from its aroma and flavor, it should be chopped only immediately before serving. Parsley is rich in iron, calcium and vitamins and aids the digestion; it may be converted into juice for drinking raw with the aid of an electric juicer. Parsley tea is particularly effective as a mild sedative and diuretic. Infuse 1 oz (25 g) of parsley leaves in 2½ cups (600 ml) of freshly boiled water for 10 minutes. It can be sweetened by the addition of honey.

MINT (Menthe) has been used in cooking and medicine for thousands of years. This most aromatic of plants was greatly valued by the Ancient Greeks and Romans and, according to myth, a nymph called Menthe – who was greatly loved by Pluto – was transformed into the herb by Prosperina, Pluto's jealous wife.

In the Middle Ages, mint – in particular pennyroyal – was an important and effective strewing herb, doing much to disguise the dreadful

ambient odors, and to repel insects. Its stimulant and digestive properties were recognized even then, and Gerard says of it, "The smell rejoiceth the heart of man, for which they caused to strew it in chambers and places of recreation, pleasure and repose where feasts and banquets are made."

When the Pilgrim Fathers sailed to America, mint was listed as one of the plants that they took with them and wherever the settlers went in the new land, the plant went too.

There are many varieties of mint, from the large woolly-leaved apple mint to the tiny intensely aromatic Corsican mint. To give a general classification of the different mints, there are the spearmints (*M. spicata*), which are used in cooking, peppermints (*M. piperata*), which are used medicinally, and the highly aromatic and decorative mints such as eau de Cologne mint (*M. citrata*), variegated apple mint (*M. rotundifolia variegata*) and ginger mint (*M. gentilis variegata*), which are attractive garden plants, ideal for pots pourris and other aromatic uses. Although not particularly decorative, pennyroyal (*M. pulegium*) falls into this last category.

Mint prefers a light, moist soil in partial shade, but as it is apt to run rampant, care must be taken to confine it, by either planting it in a container or in an area where it cannot spread unchecked. If you have the space you should try to grow three varieties of mint, a well-flavored spearmint for cooking, peppermint for tisanes, and one of the aromatic mints for fragrance. Where space is limited, the Corsican mint (*M. requienii*) will deliver the maximum aromatic impact in a small area.

So far as its medicinal qualities are concerned, the essential oil of peppermint should be used with caution in aromatherapy, and in very small quantities as it can irritate the skin.

The use of mint in cookery is universal. In India, soothing raita, a delicious combination of yoghurt, cucumber and mint, is a cooling accompaniment to curries. In the Middle East, mint and parsley are vital ingredients of tabbouleh, a refreshing, cracked wheat salad. The best Greek moussaka I have ever tasted was strongly flavored with mint and throughout Europe the herb is used in savory and sweet cooking.

For friends who enjoy cooking and gardening, mint can provide a practical and versatile present. Pot up three different mints: one could contain a culinary mint with a label giving a favorite mint recipe, another could hold a medicinal mint with a recipe for a mint tea. The third could be an aromatic mint for inclusion in a sachet or potpourri.

Nor be the little space forgot
For herbs to spice the kitchen pot;
Mint, pennyroyal, bergamot,
Tarragon and melilot,
Dill for witchcraft, prisoner's rue,
Coriander, costmary,
Tansy, thyme, Sweet Cicely,
Saffron, balm and rosemary.

THE LAND
Vita Sackville-West (1892–1962)

LEMON BALM (*Melissa officinalis*) is an aromatic plant whose Latin name is derived from the Greek word for 'bee', because it is a favourite of these insects. It was grown in monastery and cottage gardens alike for culinary and medicinal uses and was a popular strewing herb. Lemon balm was one of the primary ingredients of Eau de Carmes – a medieval cosmetic and cure-all first made in 1379.

In the garden, lemon balm is very easy to grow, and at its best in early spring. As it gets rather straggly later on, it is best planted amongst other plants which will take over in the summer.

Young lemon balm leaves are delicious in fruit drinks and fruit salads and give a lovely subtle lemon flavor to soft cheeses, as in this recipe for *coeur à la crème*.

What finer ending to a romantic dinner than coeur à la crème? This delicately flavored, sweetened cheese can be served in individual dishes for the more restrained or as one large heart with two spoons for the bold.

Coeur à la crème

This simple cheese is a blend of cream, fromage frais and egg whites, lightly sweetened with sugar. When moulding the cheese, it can be given a subtle and unusual flavor by laying a lemon balm, rose geranium or young blackcurrant leaf on top of the cheese. With its muslin covering, it is a ready-wrapped gift in itself, although it is probably best to replace the damp muslin with a fresh, dry square. Embellish it by tying on a sprig of herb or a flower.

Small, heart-shaped *coeur à la crème* moulds are available from good cookery shops. They have drainage holes in the base through which the whey will drain.

Muslin: 8 in (20 cm) square for small moulds, 12 in (30 cm) square for large moulds

2 small (3½ in [9 cm] wide) or 1 large (5 in [12 cm] wide) heart-shaped mould

2½ oz (65 g) double cream

1 egg white

8 oz (225 g) fromage frais

2 tsp caster sugar

Lemon balm, rose geranium or young blackcurrant leaves

To serve: strawberries and cream

Serves 2

Dampen the muslin squares and line the dishes. Whip the cream into soft peaks. Whip the egg white to soft peaks. Gently fold all the ingredients together. Spoon into the mould(s), and fold the muslin over the surface. Stand at room temperature for 3–4 hours during which time most of the whey will drain off. Peel back the muslin and decorate the surface with your chosen herb. Cover again with the muslin and place in the refrigerator overnight. Peel back the muslin, gently unmould the cheese and serve on a plate, surrounded with strawberries; serve with cream, if you wish.

LEMONS (Citrus) are always piled high in a large bowl in my kitchen. Their ability to enhance nearly everything they come into contact with gives them an almost alchemical quality and makes them a central player in the aromatic repertoire.

Lemons made their way to the Mediterranean from the Far East with other citrus fruit around 300 BC, but because of their acidity their use was originally limited to medicinal and ceremonial purposes. The Romans believed that the lemon was a powerful poison antidote and a type of lemon called an "etrog" has long been an important part of the Jewish Feast of the Tabernacles.

As the centuries passed, lemons were increasingly used. Oil was extracted from the skin and used in medicines, perfumes and soaps; the juice and zest were used in cooking and in cosmetics, and with the introduction of sugar, candied peel became an important sweetmeat. The Portuguese were the first to use lemons to ward off scurvy and by the middle of the 18th century, the law required that every English ship of the Royal Navy carry sufficient lemon or lime juice for every sailor to have an ounce daily after ten days at sea, a law which remained in force until the first half of the 20th century.

Lemon trees are not difficult to grow, although in a cold climate they do need winter protection and are best grown in pots. The orangeries of northern Europe were developed, as their name suggests, to cater for the needs of the citrus trees. These beautiful structures provided winter homes for the trees, which were then transferred outside into the formal gardens during the milder months. This is still the best way to look after a citrus tree in a hostile climate. Meyers lemons are particularly good in pots and can produce their first fruit at two years old. One of the great beauties of citrus trees is that they simultaneously bear fruit and flowers, but do beware – they are prone to attack from scale insects which deposit a sticky secretion and a sooty mold on the leaves. Treat promptly with a proprietary insecticide or by wiping the leaves and stems carefully with cotton wool soaked in methylated spirits, or the tree will start to lose its leaves.

In the kitchen, lemons have myriad uses. Fresh slices will enhance black teas, soft and alcoholic drinks – even water; the juice will lift a sauce and give a tang to a marinade, while the zest and peel are important flavorings in baking.

Pickled lemons

The Moroccans like to preserve lemons by pickling. This is easy enough to do and they become a marvellous ingredient for stews and will transform a simple roast chicken into an exceptional dish. When using pickled lemons, rinse them under a cold tap, remove and discard the flesh, slice the skin and add to the dish 5 minutes before it is ready. A jar of pickled lemons looks marvelous as well as tasting delicious. It makes a perfect present for gourmet friends; add a label with instructions on how to use the contents and include a recipe, too.

8–10 unwaxed lemons

¼ cup (50 g) sea salt

Extra lemon juice

2 bay leaves

2 cinnamon sticks

10 black peppercorns

Sterilized preserving jar

Gift packaging, optional

Cut a cross three-quarters through each of the lemons. Sprinkle a generous amount of salt on to the cut surfaces and push the lemons closed. Pack the lemons firmly into the jar, pressing them down as you work. Push the cinnamon sticks, peppercorns and bay leaves down among the lemons. Top up the jar with lemon juice and seal. Leave it to stand in a cool place for approximately three weeks, giving it a gentle shake from time to time. Store in the refrigerator once the jar has been opened.

Lemons have preservative qualities that make them an excellent base ingredient for aromatic flavorings to give as gifts. **Lemon vinegar** is softer and more aromatic than a plain wine vinegar and is made by pouring hot vinegar over unwaxed lemon peel and leaving it to steep for two weeks before straining and then bottling. **Lemon sugar** will give a subtle hint of lemons to cakes, sauces and custards. Remove the zest from two lemons and leave it to stand until it has dried out. Stir the zest into 1 cup (225 g) of caster sugar and seal in a glass jar. **Lemon vodka** is easy to make. Remove the outer peel from half a large unwaxed lemon, avoiding any white membrane. Leave to infuse at room temperature for no longer than 24 hours in half a bottle of vodka.

These pickled lemons look and taste wonderfully exotic, but are easily made with ingredients readily on hand. They make an impressive gift, especially when accompanied with some recipe suggestions.

Although these days lemons are used primarily for culinary purposes, you should not neglect their other qualities. Rubbed over a chopping board, a cut lemon will remove the taint of onion or garlic, it will also burnish tarnished brass and copper and will remove stains from your hands and soften and bleach roughened skin.

A simple beauty treatment for a neglected part of the body is to save used lemon halves and rest your elbows in them while you read the newspaper or watch the television.

Even today, when, it seems, the drugstores have a proprietary cure for every type of cold and cough, the tried and trusted (and cheap) combination of lemon juice and honey diluted with hot water remains an effective, safe remedy.

In aromatherapy, lemon oil is both antiseptic and antibacterial and is included in blends for the treatment of sore throats, tension headaches and insect bites. It has a tonic and astringent effect and stimulates the lymphatic system, but as it is a skin irritant, it should be used at a one per cent dilution in massage oil, or three drops to a bath. Do not use on babies or small children.

Even when the air is still chilly outside, citrus potpourri will bring the fresh scents of spring indoors. Display it in a wide bowl to allow the fragrance to permeate the room. Keep it out of direct sunlight so that the colors do not fade.

Citrus potpourri

The season is light, fresh and green and this citrus potpourri echoes that mood. Most of the ingredients can be dried at home and you should only need to buy the oils, the gum benzoin, coriander seeds and dried lemon grass.

2 oz (50 g) dried marigold petals
2 oz (50 g) dried lemon verbena leaves
1 oz (25 g) dried lemon grass
1 oz (25 g) dried lemon peel
1 oz (25 g) dried grated lemon rind
1 oz (25 g) coriander seeds
1 oz (25 g) gum benzoin (fixative)
15 drops lime essential oil
10 drops lemon essential oil
5 drops rose geranium essential oil
5 drops bergamot essential oil
4 sprigs dried mimosa
5–10 dried daffodil or narcissus heads
2–3 pieces dried orange peel
Makes approximately 9 oz (250 g) of potpourri

Mix the marigold petals, lemon verbena leaves, lemon peel and lemon grass in a large china bowl. Place the lemon rind, coriander seeds and gum benzoin in a mortar and grind thoroughly. Add the oils to the mixture in the mortar and blend well. Combine the two mixtures together in the large bowl. Store in a lidded dish and stir twice a week. Allow six weeks for the mixture to cure. To display, pour the potpourri into a wide dish and scatter with mimosa, daffodils and orange peel.

Healing herbal ointment

Spring may be here, but it can be very chilly in the garden, especially when your hands get cold, and painful cracks and rough skin are unattractive and uncomfortable. Use this ointment for any small cuts or scratches on the hands, and for a real therapeutic treatment apply generously before bedtime, putting on a pair of white cotton gloves and leaving the ointment to work overnight. This old-fashioned ointment is just the thing to give to an enthusiastic gardener, packaged in an attractive pottery container alongside, perhaps, a pair of new gardening gloves.

1 oz (25 g) lanolin
½ oz (12 g) white beeswax
3 oz (75 g) almond oil
2 fl oz (50 ml) purified water
10 drops lavender essential oil
5 drops eucalyptus essential oil
5 drops rosemary essential oil
Gift packaging, optional

Gently melt the lanolin and beeswax in a small enamel bowl over hot water. Using a hand-held electric whisk, slowly add the almond oil. Again, using the whisk, gradually incorporate the water. The mixture will emulsify and make a smooth ointment. Add the three essential oils. Pour into a glass screw-top jar or a pottery pot with a lid. Label clearly whether it is for home use or as a gift.

Chests of fragrant medicinal balm
To work cool ointments for the grieve'd flesh

Charles Jeremiah Wells (c. 1800–79)

Use this healing hand ointment to repair the ravages of gardening. Accompanied by gardening gloves and a nail brush, friends will be able to cherish their hands as well as their gardens.

Scented bath bags

After all the exertions of spring cleaning and working in the garden, it's time to treat yourself to a relaxing bath. These aromatic bath bags will help ease tired muscles and soften the skin. All you need to do is to hang a bath sachet from the hot tap so that when the water is run, it will pour over the bag and release the fragrance. You can continue to use the bag until the fragrance is no longer evident. Alternatively, if you have a lemon tree, simply pick two or three leaves and crush them in your hand before floating them in the bath for a gentle and soothing fragrance.

For a pretty and practical gift, pop several bags into a Shaker-style box or wicker basket, with an arrangement of sea shells; include a decorative card giving the principal ingredients and instructions for use.

1 oz (25 g) rolled oats

1 oz (25 g) dried lavender

1 oz (25 g) dried lemon balm or lemon verbena leaves

½ oz (15 g) dried orange peel

½ oz (15 g) dried lemon peel

2 dried bay leaves

2 dried rosemary sprigs

8 small muslin bags made from fabric 8 × 6 in (20 × 15 cm)

String

Gift boxes/baskets and shells, optional

Makes 8 bags

In a large bowl mix the oats, lavender and lemon balm or lemon verbena leaves. Using a mortar and pestle lightly crush the orange and lemon peel and the bay leaves and add to the mixture in the bowl. Break up the sprigs of rosemary and add to the mixture. Divide the mixture between the eight bags and fasten them with string.

Package the bags as described for a gift, or keep stored in a box or tin to retain their fragrance.

Ideal for a busy friend. Include instructions which explain that to gain the maximum benefit from these bath bags one should stay in the bath for at least 15 minutes with the door locked and no cordless phone at hand!

Beeswax polish

Many years ago, I bought a beautifully proportioned, but rather battered, old chest of drawers for next to nothing. I spent hours stripping away the brown varnish to reveal the original pine and then many more hours polishing it with fragrant beeswax polish. All the effort was amply rewarded and now this piece of furniture is my pride and joy, only needing the occasional application of polish to keep it glowing. These days, in our busy lives, we rarely have time for such diligence, but a special piece of furniture deserves more than a quick whizz over with a spray can and this aromatic polish is perfect for the job.

Pack the polish into a faceted jar or a pretty tin. Wrap in a duster and tie with a bow: perfect for a friend with antique furniture.

1 tbsp non-concentrated liquid lemon
dish detergent
⅔ cup (150 ml) boiling water
2 oz (50 g) beeswax
½ oz (10 g) white wax
1¼ cups (300 ml) turpentine
5 drops lemon essential oil
5 drops lavender essential oil

Makes approximately 2 cups (500 ml)

Dilute detergent in boiling water; cool. Slowly melt waxes with turpentine in a double boiler over very low heat. Take care that wax does not get hot enough to flare up. Pour soapy water into waxes, whisking well to form an emulsion. Stir in essential oils. Store in wide-neck jars with screw-top lids.

When you feel a touch of spring cleaning fever, reach for these homemade creams and polishes to enliven your furniture.

Furniture reviver

Even the most reluctant of us (I include myself here) are sometimes touched by spring fever and find ourselves cleaning the house in a most uncharacteristically thorough way. If you discover yourself similarly afflicted, I can recommend this furniture reviver as a very effective way of simultaneously polishing and removing dingy polish from neglected furniture.

Make up a cleaning kit with a jar of beeswax polish and some yellow dusters and give to a houseproud friend; it keeps indefinitely.

1 cup (200 ml) turpentine
1 cup (200 ml) linseed oil
1 cup (200 ml) malt vinegar
2 tsp granulated sugar
Gift packaging, optional

Makes 3 cups (600 ml)

Pour all the ingredients into a bottle, shake well and label clearly. To use, apply with a soft cloth. It will soften dirty polish which can then be wiped away. Polish with a clean cloth.

summer

Speak not – whisper not;
Here bloweth thyme and bergamot;
Softly on the evening hour,
Secret herbs their spices shower,
Dark-spiked rosemary and myrrh,
Lean-stalked, purple lavender;
Hides within her bosom, too,
All her sorrows bitter rue.

THE SUNKEN GARDEN
Walter de la Mare (1873–1956)

Who is not nostalgic for the summers of their childhood? Those seemingly endless, carefree days when life was simpler and the sun always shone in a cloudless blue sky. The reality may have been different, those special days may have been few and far between but, if so, this is a most benign trick of memory.

We all have certain scents that send us hurtling back to those halcyon days; for me they are the exotic perfumes of my sub-tropical childhood in South Africa – the stunningly scented frangipani and beautiful delicacy of the evergreen shrub *Brunfelsia*, which is called the "yesterday, today and tomorrow bush" because its flowers open a deep blue, fading to pale blue on the second day and, finally, white on the third. We had a bush outside our home and its scent would literally stop me in my tracks.

Living now in a more temperate climate, where the seasons are more marked, I relish the differences, and if summer sunshine is less certain, it is also infinitely more precious and its scented air is different, but no less rich.

My kitchen has French windows leading on to a sunny, stone terrace filled with pots of aromatic herbs and scented plants. This was a long-held dream which was finally realized when I moved to my current house and it means that I can benefit from every moment of sunshine, flinging wide the doors and allowing the scents of roses, jasmine, honeysuckle, lilies and lavender to drift in.

In the kitchen, fresh herbs make feasts of the simplest dishes, which is fortunate, for this is not

the time to spend long hours indoors. Instead, young leaves and vegetables are made into salads or lightly cooked and served in the evening sun in the backyard. Paradise regained.

Many of the sun-loving plants of the summer garden are richly aromatic and it is tempting to plant every one that appeals to you, but some discipline is needed or the garden can become a kaleidoscopic muddle. There are very few natural

This is the season of clove-scented pinks, frothy Queen Anne's lace, heady garden roses and fragrant sweet peas.

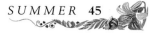

the buff-apricot 'Gloire de Dijon' and the clear pink 'Constance Spry'. Intermingle the roses with jasmine, honeysuckle and in milder areas the scented passionflower 'Incana', and the evergreen star jasmine (*Trachelospermum jasminoides*).

The border should include fragrant flowers for picking such as peonies, bergamot, sweet peas, lilies, pinks and lavender. A sunny, paved area is ideal for aromatic herbs and pots of scented plants such as *Salvia rutilans*, with its aroma of pineapples, and the blackcurrant-scented *S. discolor*.

Now is the time to move plants outside from windowsills and greenhouses. Pot-grown citrus trees will bloom profusely and spread their glorious scent in the warm air, *Datura* will release its narcotic fragrance to the night and scented geraniums spice the air with rose, lemon and pine.

Each year, in June, I visit a flower farm where I buy peonies for drying. There, the gorgeous, blowsy blooms stand in buckets of water in the dim light of a cold room. Before my eyes can adjust to the light and appreciate the sight of thousands of these beautiful flowers, I am transported by their fragrance – one of the most beautiful that I know. It is light, spicy and lemony at the same time and particularly precious for being so transient; even today when tulips can be bought in October and roses in January, peonies have their brief few weeks of glory in early summer and then disappear until the following year. I always buy more than I need for drying so that for one glorious week of unrivalled olfactory pleasure, I can fill my home with a surfeit of peonies.

scents which do not blend harmoniously in the open air, so the discipline should be visual rather than olfactory. Decide on a color scheme, and stick to it for most of your planting.

Create structure with trees and shrubs; if there is room, include lilac, philadelphus, buddleia and broom, all wonderfully fragrant and much appreciated by bees and butterflies. On walls and fences, plant scented roses such as the deep red 'Guinee',

In the garden, there is a fragrant abundance, not only of scented roses, precious lilies and trailing honeysuckle, but also wonderfully aromatic foliage, in particular southernwood, also known as lad's love (it was once the habit of young men to wear a sprig of it in their lapels when they went courting). The addition of aromatic herbs such as southernwood, rosemary or lemon verbena will enliven a flower arrangement and scent the room.

Summer posy

Unlike the compact and symmetrical Spring Posy (page 18), I like summer versions to be looser and very informal. When I make one of these posies, I wander around the garden picking flowers that catch my eye and reflect my mood.

With this type of posy, don't try to make the arrangement symmetrical – part of its charm is that it looks "just picked" rather than carefully planned. Even if you don't have your own garden, it is possible to create an informal posy by buying your flowers from a florist where you can select single stems rather than whole bunches of flowers.

Take a summer posy and a pretty vase as a present when invited to friends for dinner. Your thoughtfulness will be appreciated as your hosts are relieved of the task of finding a vase and arranging a bunch of flowers while trying to serve dinner and engage in witty conversation.

It is worth growing the old-fashioned sweet peas; the flowers are not so large, but the scent is far stronger. A posy of sweet peas and lady's mantle (*Alchemilla mollis*) is a lovely summer gift.

Many of the most fragrant roses have heavy heads that tend to droop in flower arrangements; this makes them far more suitable for informal arranging, such as a pretty jug of full-blown roses or a posy where other flowers can support them.

Selection of summer flowers and foliage

Twine

Ribbon

Condition the flowers as follows: trim the stems, strip back any foliage at the end of the stems and stand them in deep water in a cool place for a couple of hours. Begin to select flowers and assemble your posy, holding it loosely in one hand and rearranging it as necessary until you are happy with the overall effect. The central flowers should be higher than those towards the outside of the posy and you should incorporate some foliage, especially towards the outside of the posy, which will help to conceal the stems.

Bind the stems firmly with twine and trim the stems to the same length using a pair of scissors. Add a matching ribbon or a twist of foliage to conceal the twine.

The hot colors of the red and pink roses and phlox in this posy are intensified by the contrasting lime green of the dill, to make a highly aromatic combination. Dill is a wonderful addition to summer flower arrangements with its feathery foliage and star-burst flowers.

Pot-et-fleur

Mixing foliage pot plants and cut flowers was very popular in Victorian times, but is less so these days. This is a pity, as it is an easy and effective way of creating lovely arrangements which are ideal as centerpieces for a formal dinner party or a celebratory meal. By replacing the cut flowers, the arrangement will last long beyond the event.

A *pot-et-fleur* is a beautiful gift which needs no further embellishment. Include instructions on how to revive the arrangement with fresh flowers and how best to care for the ferns. (Maidenhair ferns thrive on a regular feed of chopped up banana skins!)

3 blocks of green florists' foam
Large bowl or similar suitable watertight container
3 maidenhair ferns in pots
10 stems of white lilies
20 long-stemmed white freesias
10 stems of Queen Anne's lace

Soak the florists' foam in water until it is saturated. Position the maidenhair ferns in the bowl ensuring that some of the foliage tumbles over the sides. Fill all the spaces between the pots with pieces of foam cut to shape.

Trim the stems of the lilies and push them into the foam so that the flowers nestle among the ferns. Fill in with the freesias and Queen Anne's lace. Add more water if the foam dries out, but don't overwater or the ferns will rot.

This mix of potted plants and cut flowers is perfect for summer gifts or celebrations and has the advantage that the addition of the flowers can be done at the last moment.

LAVENDER *(Lavandula)* – much prized in Ancient Greece – was known as "nard" after the Syrian city of Naarda. It may be that this plant is the nard referred to in The Song of Soloman and in the New Testament when Mary Magdalene used nard to anoint Christ's feet and was reviled by those around her for using such a precious substance. The Romans perfumed their baths with it, and it is possible that the name lavender is a derivative of the Latin word *lavare*, to wash. Lavender is undoubtedly a plant that has long been considered to be of the greatest importance for its aromatic and healing properties.

The practice of using lavender to perfume linen dates from medieval times and may well have been adopted as much for lavender's insect repelling properties as for its penetrating fragrance. The 17th-century English writer Izaak Walton clearly recognized quality lodgings when he wrote, 'Let's go to that house, for the linen looks white and smells of lavender and I long to be in a pair of sheets that smell so.'

Lavender was also an important strewing herb, and was much used in cooking for savory and sweet purposes alike. It was an alternative to mint in stews, the flowers were used in salads and candied as sweets, and it was also a key ingredient in cordials, preserves and syrups.

Lavender sugar was a very popular flavoring for cakes and cookies or to make a lavender ice cream. You can make it by pounding three parts of sugar to one of lavender flowers. A simpler method is to layer the same quantities of sugar and lavender in a screw-top glass jar. After a couple of weeks, sift the sugar to remove the flowers as the aroma will have transferred to the sugar.

In the stillrooms of bygone days, lavender was used to make pots pourris and "to perfume linnen, apparell, gloves and leather and the dried flowers to comfort and dry up the moisture of a cold braine." Lavender remains as important an ingredient in today's perfume industry as it was in the past. As well as being used as a perfume and cosmetic it was also taken as a medicine.

It is only in fairly recent times that the alcohol in perfume has been de-natured, making it unsuitable for internal use.

Lavender is one of the major essential oils used in aromatherapy. It is antibacterial, antidepressant, anti-fungal, anti-inflammatory, antiseptic, antiviral, a deodorant and an insect repellent. Lavender is effective for skin complaints, burns and cuts and can alleviate migraine.

Here's your sweet Lavender,
sixteen sprigs a penny,
Which you'll find, my ladies,
will smell as sweet as any.

Traditional 'Cries of London'

Lavender is a great reviver of spirits and lavender water is a refreshing gift for the oppressive dog days of summer. Its scent conjures up images of Victorian ladies in white lace gowns, but thanks to aromatherapy it is experiencing a renaissance of renewed popularity.

Lavender water

Lavender water was at its most popular in the last century, when ladies carried scented handkerchiefs to revive flagging spirits and relieve nervous headaches. It became known as an "old ladies' scent," but with the recent surge of interest in aromatherapy, it is regaining popularity. Use it as a room spray, pour some in your bath or dip a handkerchief in cooled lavender water and pat on the face and neck to relieve a headache.

For a pretty gift, look out for antique scent bottles to fill with lavender water and use purple ribbon to attach a label.

⅓ cup (100 ml) vodka
2⅓ cups (600 ml) bottle
10 drops lavender essential oil
2 cups (500 ml) distilled water
Gift packaging: antique scent bottles, ribbons optional

Makes 2⅓ cups (600 ml)

Pour the vodka into the bottle. Add the lavender oil. Top up the bottle with the water and shake to mix. For maximum cooling effect, store in the refrigerator. Lavender water keeps indefinitely.

ROSES *(Rosa)* have long held a place in our hearts. The forebears of the modern rose can be traced to Persia and the East, and from the very beginning, roses have been valued for their beauty and fragrance. The word rose comes from the Greek word for red – *rodon* – and the Ancient Greeks and Romans were enthusiastic cultivators of the flower. Horace writes of growing roses in beds and Pliny advises deep cultivation for best results. The Romans, too, were obsessed with roses, fountains were filled with rosewater, pillows stuffed with rose petals and they even ate rose puddings.

The Persians, who were the first to learn how to extract oils from flowers by distillation (between 1582 and 1612), became expert perfume makers. It is said that the existence of flower oils was first discovered at the wedding feast of Princess Noor Jihan. A canal was dug to surround the garden and filled with rosewater. As the happy couple rowed on the canal they observed a film of oil which the heat of the sun had separated from the rosewater. Trailing their hands in the water they found it to be the finest perfume. Shortly afterwards, the first distilleries were set up in Shiraz and the first rose oil or attar of roses was produced.

The Renaissance brought the appreciation of fine fragrances and the process of distillation to Europe. As part of the perfume industry, plantations of roses and other flowers were established around Grasse in the south of France. Production continues to this day, although now the only attar of roses that is produced there is for the French perfume house Chanel, and the world's major producers are now Bulgaria and Turkey. One acre of roses produces only around ten pounds of attar in a season.

Historically, the rose has been a symbol of secrecy, and it was traditional to suspend a rose above a dinner table to indicate that all that was said would be in confidence or *sub rosa*. This is the origin of the decorative plaster "rose" on ceilings in period houses.

As well as being a central ingredient in perfumes, roses were used domestically in huge quantities for making syrups, jams, cordials and sugars for both culinary and medicinal purposes.

Rose sugar is also a delicious flavoring, and although very few of us have access to sufficient numbers of well-scented, deep red roses, a jar of rose sugar requires quite modest quantities and is a delicious flavoring in cakes, custards and sorbets, especially if you include some good-quality rosewater with the other ingredients.

Rose sugar

Only use roses that you know have not been sprayed with chemicals, and select them for their strong scent. Ideally, they should be picked in the middle of the morning, after any moisture has disappeared, but before the sun becomes too hot and evaporates the volatile oils. For a scented gift, pack a jar of rose sugar and a bottle of rosewater in a pretty box with some suggestions on how to use them.

2 oz (50 g) deep red rose petals
1 cup (225 g) castor sugar
Glass screw-top jar
Gift packaging, optional

Layer the roses and sugar evenly in the jar. Close the jar and leave in a warm place for up to two weeks for the flavor to develop. Sieve the sugar before use to remove the petals, which can be a bit tough.

During the first half of this century, the main concern of rose breeders was to develop varieties which flowered all summer long, and fragrance was often sacrificed to this cause. Fortunately, this is no longer the case and now there are many wonderfully fragrant modern roses which are also repeat flowering – and any good-quality rose catalogue will have a wide selection suitable for all sizes of garden.

For the purists, the fragrance of old roses is incomparable, but they do flower for a relatively short period. For those with space I would recommend the apothecary's rose (*Rosa gallica officinalis*) and the Provence rose (*R. centifolia*) as two of the oldest cultivated roses renowned for their fragrance. Recent trials of old roses, to establish the most fragrant for rose oil production, finally chose four varieties: 'Belle de Crecy', 'Louis Odier', 'Madame Isaac Pereire' and 'Roseraie de L'Hay'.

A variety of scented products derived from roses is available. Attar of roses, also known as rose otto, is obtained by steam distillation and is the

While most of us are familiar with vanilla sugar, few will have used flower sugars, which is a great pity as they can add an intriguing extra dimension. Rose sugar will impart a subtle flavor to sorbets, custards and creams.

finest pure rose oil. Rosewater is generally a by-product from the distillation process of attar of roses. The best rosewater is triple distilled. Buy culinary quality rosewater rather than any in perfume-type bottles, as the latter may be inferior. Nowadays some flower waters are obtained by "washing" the petals in alcohol (isopropanol) and then diluting the mixture with distilled water. Rose absolute, obtained by bathing the petals in a volatile solvent, is not as highly regarded as rose otto when used for therapeutic purposes.

Because pure rose oil is prohibitively expensive, all rose essential oils are a dilution of either rose otto or rose absolute with other oils. Buy the best that you can afford from a reputable company. Some of the cheapest rose oils are totally synthetic and have no therapeutic effect. In aromatherapy, rose oil is good at calming strong emotions and relieving stress; it is helpful for chest complaints, poor circulation and is also considered an aphrodisiac. Add three or four drops to a bath for energy, and a touch of euphoria!

Softly scented rosebuds are tightly packed together to make fragrant rose balls which can be used to scent drawers and cupboards or simply displayed as lovely decorative objects.

Scented rose ball

The rose ball is a simple interpretation of a medieval pomander and is a lovely alternative to today's synthetic room fragrancers. Rosebuds can be obtained from botanical suppliers and herbalists, though you may find that you need to buy large quantities. Alternatively, shops selling ingredients for potpourri generally sell packets of rosebuds and I find this a fairly economical way to buy them. The roses have a gentle scent of their own, but it is very subtle, so I use some rose essential oil to enhance the fragrance. (When working with dry foam and essential oils be careful not to touch your eyes, as both can irritate.)

As a pretty gift, package the pomander in a decorative box, nestling within tissue paper. When the lid of the box is lifted, the wonderful scent will be released.

3 in (7 cm) diameter dry foam ball
Rose essential oil
1¾ yd (1.5 m) of ½ in (12 mm) wide ribbon
Pins
2 oz (60 g) rosebuds
All-purpose glue
Gift packaging, optional

Make a small hole in the foam ball and release 6–8 drops of rose oil into it. Cut the ribbon into two equal lengths and tie them round the ball, effectively dividing it into quarters. (It may help to pin them in place before fastening.)

Dip the base of each rosebud into the glue (each one has a small stalk which can be pushed right into the foam). Stud the quarters with the rosebuds and pack them closely together so that no foam is visible.

SCENTED GERANIUMS (*Pelargonium*) are more subtle than the traditional geraniums which bear showy, scarlet flowers. While these plants of summer do have a pungent, spicy scent that instantly conjures up blue skies and hot, dry days, there are many other varieties with scents ranging from peppermint through nutmeg and pine to balsam and lilac. The best known of these scented plants is the lemon-scented, oak leaf geranium, which is popular as an ingredient for potpourris and can be used as a culinary flavoring. My best results have been obtained by infusing the leaves in water or cream and then using the infusion to flavor ice creams, custards or sorbets.

Pelargonium capitatum, *P. graveolens* and *P. odoratissimum* are the source of geranium essential oils which are particularly good to use in diffusers to scent rooms, in a massage oil for relief of stress and anxiety, or in face and body lotions.

An unusual present for the visually impaired (especially if you can arrange for braille plant labels) is to pot a selection of scented-leaf geraniums in weathered terracotta and label each plant, giving its name and its fragrance.

Geranium cream is a deliciously rich pudding made with cream, cream cheese and fromage frais. Serve just a spoonful with raspberries or loganberries or even as an accompaniment to summer pudding. Scoop into an attractive dish to take to a summer party.

Geranium cream

This subtle-flavored creamy dessert makes the perfect summertime pudding. and one to take to a friend's barbecue party.

5 fl oz (150 ml) fromage frais
5 fl oz (150 ml) double cream
4 tbsp caster sugar
3 scented geranium leaves
6 oz (175 g) cream cheese
Serves 8–10

Place the cream, sugar and geranium leaves in the top of a double boiler and heat gently until the sugar dissolves and the cream is hot. Leave to cool and add the fromage frais. Stir this mixture into the cream cheese. Chill overnight. Before serving remove the geranium leaves.

Nothing is more gracious than the Lily in
fairness of color, in sweetnesse of smell,
and in effect of working or vertue.

Bartholomaeus Anglicus
(13th century scholar)

LILIES (Lilium) are an essential ingredient in the scented summer garden with their wonderful waxy blooms and their heady scent. Among the most fragrant are the madonna lily (*Lilium candidum*) – ideal in the border under rosemary and lavender – and *L. regale* , which should be placed in pots near doors and windows so that you can easily appreciate their delicious scent. Of the modern hybrids, the 'Casablanca' lily has a particularly fine scent and very beautiful large white flowers.

The lily has long been a Christian symbol. The flower's combination of fertility and purity led to its association with the Annunciation, and for centuries paintings always included a lily held by the madonna or the angel. In Cyprus, to this day, any young girl who becomes pregnant outside marriage is said to have "sniffed the lily."

In the Middle Ages, lily roots were ground up with herbs and vinegar to make a stomach poultice, and were used in the same way to treat boils and burns. Lily root syrup was used for colic and pleurisy, and lily snuff was used as a decongestant until the last century. Today, the lily is not used medicinally, but it remains one of the most popular flowers for fragrance and decoration and an inspiration to poets and painters alike.

Even the smallest garden can have a scented corner
with the addition of pots of fragrant flowers. Lilies
and jasmine both thrive in pots and fill the garden
with their delicious scent.

JASMINE *(Jasminum)* emits one of the most seductive aromas of summer. The common jasmine (*Jasminum officinale*) is a rampant grower which will quickly cover a wall or shed and is best left unpruned. For warmer areas, there are tender jasmines such as *J. angulare* from southern Africa and *J. sambac*, the Arabian jasmine, which both flower almost continuously if warm enough.

Jasmine first came to the West when the Moors brought it to the Spanish peninsula from Persia around 720 AD. It proved to be an adaptable plant which grew well, so that by the time Culpeper wrote his *Herbal* in the 17th century he refers to the use of fragrant "Jessamine" oil for perfumes and its ability "to disperse crude humours."

Along with roses, jasmine was, and still is, one of the primary crops grown for the perfume industry around Grasse in the south of France. The fragrance of the jasmine grown here is quite different from that raised in other parts of the world. It is more balanced, cool and narcotic and is believed to be the very finest. By contrast, jasmine oil from flowers grown, for example, in India and Egypt is less subtle. All the jasmine now grown in Grasse is for use in Chanel No. 5, which contains ten per cent jasmine oil. The perfume house has no option but to support the growers in the area as oil from another source would perceptibly change the fragrance even though it would cost them one-twelfth of the locally manufactured oil. Every kilo of jasmine absolute requires four-and-a-half million hand-picked flowers!

Traditionally, the scent was removed from the jasmine flowers by a method called *enfleurage*. Lard and tallow were spread on sheets of glass in wooden frames and the flowers were then placed individually on the fat. The fat absorbed the fragrance and the flowers were replaced daily until the fat became saturated with the fragrance. Modern methods have surplanted *enfleurage*, but it can still be seen at the distilleries in Grasse.

If you have a prolific jasmine plant in your garden, you can experiment with *enfleurage* for yourself. Smear the inside surfaces of a wide-necked jar with a layer of unscented moisturizing cream. Press jasmine flowers face down into the cream and fasten the lid. Leave to stand in a warm place. Replace the flowers daily for up to a month – at the end of this time the cream should smell strongly of jasmine. Remove the flowers, stir in more cream and use as a perfumed moisturizer.

To make jasmine tea, add 1 tablespoon of dried jasmine flowers to 4 oz (110 g) of your favorite large-leafed China tea. For a tea-drinking friend, blend jasmine tea and rose petals (using similar proportions of well-scented dried rose petals) and decant into decorative jars or tins.

> *. . . and luxuriant above all*
> *The jasmine, throwing wide her elegant sweets,*
> *The deep dark green of whose unvarnished leaf*
> *Makes more conspicuous, and illumines more*
> *The bright profusion of her scattered stars.*
>
> THE TASK
> William Cowper (1731–1800)

LEMON VERBENA (Lippia citriodora) is essential in an aromatic garden, even though the plant itself is not very decorative. It should be planted on a sunny terrace or the edge of a path where you will brush against it and release its lovely fragrance. I have a plant next to the garden tap, and every time I fill a can with water I am surrounded by the delightful, piercing lemon scent. I find that I can usually keep a plant for four or five years before a particularly cold winter kills it and it needs to be replaced. In cold areas, it is best to grow lemon verbena in a pot and over-winter it in a suitable place indoors.

Lemon verbena can be used in pots pourris, and a sprig included in a syrup for poaching fruit will give a delightful perfumed lemony flavor. The scent is at its best when the plant is in flower.

Tisanes
Herb teas

In France, lemon verbena is known as verveine and is frequently drunk as a therapeutic tea or tisane. It is one of four teas that are regarded as essential home cures: verveine to aid digestion and as a mild sedative; sage for sore throats; thyme as a purifier and disinfectant; and lime for constipation and to aid sleep.

Make up packets of the four dried herbs and attach labels giving instructions on how to make the tisanes and what they can be used for.

5–6 lemon verbena leaves
(or herb of your choice)
2½ cups (600 ml) cold water
Strip of orange peel, optional
Honey to taste, optional
Gift packaging, optional

Place the leaves in the cold water and bring to the boil. Cover and remove from the heat. Add orange peel, if wished. Leave to infuse for 10 minutes, then add honey to taste.

Of all the lemon-scented herbs, I consider lemon verbena to be the finest. It makes a refreshing tea which will quench the thirst and aid digestion. Served in a tisane glass you can appreciate its lovely color.

BASIL (Ocimum basilicum) has the reputation of being the "king" of herbs, in part because its name is believed to be derived from the Greek *Vasilikos* which means "king." It is native to India, where it is sacred to Vishnu and Krishna and is believed to be the protecting spirit of the family.

The Ancient Greeks and Romans believed that it represented hate and misfortune and thought the plant would not grow unless abused when the seeds were sown.

In medieval times, a superstition grew up that linked basil with the scorpion. An English herbalist wrote "being gently handled it gave a pleasant smell, but being hardly wrung and bruised would breed scorpions." In the Mediterranean regions it was generally believed that if a sprig of basil was left under a pot it would turn into a scorpion.

Despite all this, basil became a very popular herb in Tudor England (perhaps because of an absence of scorpions in those parts) and was much used for strewing.

Supermarkets now stock basil all year round, but I firmly believe that you can never have enough of this delicious fragrant herb, so it always has a place in my summer garden. There are many different forms and it is well worth growing a selection both for variety of flavor and appearance. In my experience, basil is best sown in pots in the spring and kept on a windowsill or in a greenhouse until the weather is really warm. I then plant it out in full sun in a light, fertile soil. Pinch out the growing tips to encourage of leaf growth.

In cooking, basil enlivens all it comes in contact

with – it is a veritable herbal truffle, and like the truffle I think that it is often at its best when used in very simple dishes such as omelettes, shredded over a plate of spaghetti with curls of Parmesan, or perhaps best of all used in a salad of sun-ripened tomatoes with lots of garlic and olive oil.

Fresh tomato and basil sauce

I think of tomato and basil sauce as bottled sunshine. With a good supply in the cupboard, you will never be at a loss for a present.

Note: As this sauce contains no preservative it must be bottled into a clean, sterilized jar. Once opened, the jar should be refrigerated and the sauce used within two weeks. I also like to freeze some in ice-cube trays to add a touch more flavor to sauces and gravies.

At the height of the summer, when the tomatoes are at their most flavorsome and basil is plentiful, I like to make this sauce which I freeze for use in winter. It retains the fresh flavors and is delicious poured over vegetables, or in stews and casseroles.

½ cup (120 ml) virgin olive oil
4 medium-sized onions, finely chopped
10 large garlic cloves, chopped
6 large carrots, peeled and sliced
1 head of celery, chopped, including leaves
5 lb (2.25 kg) skinned and quartered,
very ripe tomatoes
4 large handfuls of basil
Half a bottle of red wine
Pepper and salt
4 tbsp demerara sugar
2 tbsp wine vinegar
Makes 2½ quarts (2.25 litres)

Heat the oil in a large pan and gently fry the onions over a low heat, stirring frequently until they are soft and golden. Add the garlic, cook for 1 minute and then add the chopped carrots and celery. Stir frequently until the vegetables have softened. Add the chopped tomatoes, basil, red wine, pepper and salt, bring the mixture to the boil and then leave to simmer uncovered for 2 hours. Combine the mixture in a blender. Return to the pan, add the sugar and vinegar and simmer uncovered until the sauce has reduced by half. Cool, then freeze or bottle.

Bouquets garnis

Whether made with fresh herbs or dried, the home-made bouquet garni will always be infinitely superior to the commercial variety. (Always use dried bay leaves in bouquet garni, as they have a tendency to be bitter when fresh.)

Make bundles of bouquets garnis and decorate them with a bay leaf to give as a present. Store in an airtight glass jar or tin.

FRESH BOUQUET GARNI
2 dried bay leaves
Generous sprig of fresh thyme
Large sprig of parsley
Makes one bouquet

Tie the herbs into a bundle with string, leaving a long loop for removing the bouquet garni when the dish is cooked. For richer dishes, add a strip of orange peel or a celery stalk.

DRIED BOUQUET GARNI
1 tsp dried marjoram
1 tsp dried basil
1 tsp dried thyme
1 tsp dried savory
1 dried bay leaf (crumbled)
4 black peppercorns
4 in (10 cm) square of muslin
String
Makes one bouquet

Heap the herbs in the middle of the muslin. Gather up the sides and tie the bundle firmly.

Here's flowers for you;
Hot lavender, mints, savory, marjoram
The marigold that goes to bed wi' the sun,
And with him rises weeping.

A WINTER'S TALE
William Shakespeare (1564–1616)

Don't wait until the autumn to harvest all your herbs. Dry some in mid-summer when their flavor is at its peak for use in bouquets garnis (left). Tied in muslin and decorated with a bay leaf they make an appropriate gift for town-dwelling friends. Keep fresh bouquets garnis (below) in a lidded plastic box with a damp paper towel.

OREGANO/MARJORAM (*Origanum*) is found in various forms, sometimes called marjoram and sometimes oregano, but all these herbs are in fact part of the same family.

Marjoram was widely used by the Ancient Greeks and Romans who greatly appreciated its wonderful camphorous scent. Medicinally, it was much used to counteract narcotic poisoning, for dropsy and as a poultice. In the Middle Ages, it was a popular strewing herb and was used extensively in the stillroom in the making of perfumes.

There should always be space in the garden for some marjoram. It is a fine aromatic plant for the front of a border or on the edge of paths, and when in flower it will be alive with bees.

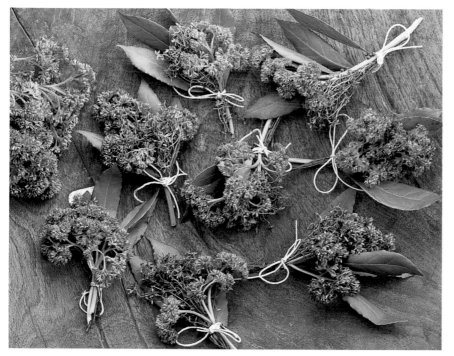

The Greek culinary herb *rigani* – which is used with lemon juice to give kebabs their characteristic flavor – is in fact made from the flowers of the wild marjoram. In Italy, the leaves are an essential seasoning for pizzas.

In aromatherapy, marjoram oil is good for headaches and sports injuries. Do not use on babies, small children, when pregnant or if you have low blood pressure.

THYME (*Thymus*) grows freely throughout Europe, from the shores of the Mediterranean to high in the Alps. Its name seems to be an adaptation of the Greek *thumon*, which meant "to fumigate" and perhaps referred to its use as a burning herb or incense. In Ancient Greece, thyme symbolized courage – *thumos* – and to be told that "one smelt of thyme" was a great compliment.

There are many varieties of thyme but only two basic types. The first is the prostrate thyme – varieties of *Thymus serpyllum* or *drucei* – which is ideal for planting among paving stones, while the bushy thyme – cultivars of *T. vulgaris* – is good planted alongside paths and at the edge of borders. Among the most fragrant thymes are *T. fragrantissimus*, with its scent which blends oranges and balsam, and *T. herba barona*, which smells of caraway. The lemon thyme (*T. × citriodorus*) is a particularly good cooking herb, but it does need shelter.

Thyme has many uses in the kitchen; lemon thyme is especially good with roast chicken, and will enliven the flavor of stews and casseroles.

Sweet pepper oil

All the summer herbs, with their high aromatic content, are good for flavoring oils and vinegars for making salad dressings and marinades. Make sure you fill the bottle to the top with oil, to cover the herbs and peppercorns.

Use a rustic basket as a gift container for bottles of aromatic oils and vinegars. Label them clearly and give directions for their use.

1 red pepper *(Capsicum)*
3 plump garlic cloves
1 cup of wine vinegar
3 good-size sprigs of rosemary
1 tsp pink peppercorns
1¼ cups (300 ml) virgin olive oil
Decorative glass bottle, sterilized
Makes 1¼ cups (300 ml)

Grill the pepper until the skin is black. Place in a plastic bag and leave for 10–15 minutes. Remove the skin and dice the flesh.

Roast the garlic cloves in their skins for 15 minutes in a hot oven, then peel.

Bring vinegar to boil and pour over rosemary sprigs and peppercorns. Leave to stand for 5 minutes. Remove rosemary and peppercorns from vinegar and drain on kitchen paper. Place rosemary, peppercorns, pepper and garlic cloves in a decorative bottle. Add oil, filling bottle right to the top, and seal it securely. Store for up to 1 week in the refrigerator. For longer periods, strain into a freezer-safe container and freeze.

Lime vinegar

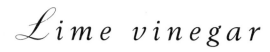 Flavored vinegars are wonderful in salad dressings or sauces. This lime vinegar is excellent in a dressing for seafood dishes. Lime leaves and lemon grass are available in packs of fresh Thai herbs from large supermarkets.

Other tasty vinegars include mint vinegar, for home-made mint sauce, and tarragon vinegar for salad dressings and hollandaise sauce.

3 limes, peeled and sliced (keep the peel)
Wide-necked jar
1⅔ cups (400 ml) white wine vinegar
Decorative bottle
1 or 2 lime leaves
1 piece of lemon grass

Place the sliced limes in the wide-necked jar. Heat 1¼ cups (300 ml) of the vinegar to boiling and pour over the limes. Cover tightly and leave to infuse overnight. Strain the vinegar and pour into the decorative bottle.

Heat the remaining vinegar to boiling and blanch the lime leaves, lemon grass and 2 or 3 strips of lime peel briefly before adding them to the lime vinegar. Seal the bottle and leave to infuse for a week.

Flavored oils and vinegars can be a single flavor like the thyme oil on the left, or a blend as in the sweet pepper oil next to it. Similarly the shallot vinegar is simply chopped shallots in red wine vinegar, while the lime vinegar makes use of lemon grass and lime leaves.

Note: *Traditionally herbs and flavorings were simply added to oils without any treatment, but it has been found that harmful molds can form. To be safe, store oils in the refrigerator and use within one week, or if the oils are for long-term use, they should be strained to remove the herbs and flavorings after one week of infusing and then store in the freezer.*

ROSEMARY (*Rosmarinus officinalis*), like lavender, has long been cultivated for its aromatic qualities and medicinal properties. Its reputation as the herb of remembrance may have some basis of truth as it is used by herbalists, even today, to treat forgetfulness. In the Middle Ages, rosemary was held in high regard and was used for a multitude of purposes. It was one of the main strewing herbs, was reputed to fend off bad dreams if kept under the bed, cure coughs, ease gout and, according to Banckes' *Herbal*: "if thou be feeble boyle the leaves in cleane water and washe thyself and thou shalt wax shiny." In Mrs. Grieve's *A Modern Herbal*, she states that rosemary branches and juniper berries were still being burnt to purify the air in French hospitals during the 1920s.

Rosemary was much used in religious ceremonies. As the symbol of remembrance, it was widely used at weddings and funerals to deck churches, and in witchcraft it was used for spells. An old French word for rosemary is *incensier*, indicating its use as a substitute for incense.

Rosemary was the central ingredient of the first perfume to be made in Europe using distillation. Hungary Water, named after Queen Elizabeth of Hungary, was based on oil of rosemary with lavender added. A formula dated 1235 and reputed to be in the queen's own handwriting is said to be in existence in Vienna.

Rosemary is native to the Mediterranean and although it is believed that the Romans introduced it to northern Europe, it is thought that it proved difficult to keep alive and that in these regions it was lost to cultivation until it was re-introduced in the 14th century. By then, more was understood of its needs and it became an important plant in every monastery garden. From there, it spread far and wide and began to enjoy a popularity which continues to this day.

Rosemary grows both as a prostrate plant and an upright one, and I like to grow both. The upright plant can become very large in time and needs a sunny sheltered spot and well-drained soil to do really well (especially, if like me, you are frequently plundering its branches for cooking and flower arrangements). The prostrate variety looks particularly good in containers or against walls where its tumbling branches can be seen to full advantage; once again it needs a position in full sun. Rosemary is such a wonderful plant that I recommend growing as many plants as you have room for, it looks marvellous among old roses and will reach a considerable height against a sunny wall.

In the kitchen, rosemary has long been a popular flavoring for roast meats, but it is also delicious roasted with potatoes, and with chicken and fish.

Rosemary essential oil is considered to invigorate, refresh and stimulate. A bath with a few drops of rosemary oil will get your day off to a good start. Inhaling rosemary-scented steam will help relieve cold symptoms and coughs. Rosemary is a powerful detoxicant and a good headache remedy. For arthritis, blend with juniper and frankincense. (Rosemary oil should never be used in pregnancy or for those with high blood pressure.)

As for Rosmarine, I lett it runne all over my garden walls, not onlie because my bees love it, but because it is the herb sacred to remembrance, and, therefore, to friendship; whence a sprig of it hath a dumb language that maketh it the chosen emblem of our funeral wakes and in our buriall grounds.

Sir Thomas More
(1478–1535)

Rosemary hair rinse

In these days when so many hair care products are available, it is a relief to use something as simple and effective as rosemary hair rinse. My daughter finds it an excellent conditioner for her thick dark hair, while I make a similar version for my fair hair, substituting chamomile flowers for the rosemary.

Give a friend who is going away a rosemary-themed gift for remembrance: a rosemary posy, a rosemary plant and a bottle of this rosemary hair rinse.

10 stems of rosemary
3½ pints (2 litres) bottled still water
½ cup (120 ml) white wine or cider vinegar
5 drops rosemary essential oil

Break the rosemary stems into short lengths and place them in a large lidded pan or bowl. Bring the water to the boil and pour over the rosemary sprigs and cover tightly. Leave to infuse for four hours.

Strain the rosemary water, add the vinegar and the essential oil and mix thoroughly. Pour into clean bottles with screw tops or corks. Label clearly.

Summer potpourri

This richly fragrant and vibrantly colored potpourri echoes the bright flowers of summer borders. Its aroma is hot and spicy, with a touch of lemon, and it will conjure up the high days of summer long after they have gone. The basic mixture of rosebuds, rose petals, lavender and lemon verbena is blended with a rich selection of spices and oils to give a deep, lasting fragrance. Display it in a wide bowl with a few flowers that echo the color theme. Purple pompon dahlias, cerise pink peonies and crimson roses are good choices.

Look for pierced silver or brass potpourri boxes in shops that stock decorative pieces. Filled with summer potpourri, they make a perfect aromatic gift.

1 oz (30 g) red rose petals

2 oz (50 g) pink rosebuds

2 oz (50 g) lavender flowers

1 oz (30 g) lemon verbena

1 tbsp allspice

1 tbsp cinnamon

1 tbsp cloves

2 tsp gum benzoin

1 oz (25 g) finely chopped oakmoss

2 tbsp (25 ml) almond oil

10 drops rose essential oil

5 drops geranium essential oil

2 drops ginger essential oil

Gift box, optional

Makes 6 oz (175 g)

Mix the dried rose petals, rosebuds, lavender and lemon verbena in a large bowl and the allspice, cinnamon, cloves, gum benzoin and oakmoss in a smaller bowl.

Blend the almond oil with the rose, geranium and ginger oils and pour it over the spice mixture, working it in thoroughly. Mix the spice and oil blend into the dried flowers.

To cure, place potpourri in a bag (not plastic) or a lidded earthenware container, shake or stir twice a week. Allow six weeks to cure.

Home-made rose potpourri is a perfect gift for a summer wedding. The fragrance will be associated with the happy day and the colors reminiscent of the summer garden. Gift wrap with some additional oil to refresh the mixture.

Florida waters

Eau de Cologne and other blended floral waters have a light fragrance that is very refreshing, especially if you keep a spray bottle of it in the refrigerator to cool you off on a hot summer's day.

Gift wrap a bottle with a pretty handkerchief.

3½ tbsp (50 ml) vodka
8 drops bergamot essential oil
8 drops lavender essential oil
2 drops clove essential oil
2 cups (500 ml) bottled still water
Makes 2¼ cups (550 ml)

Pour the vodka and oils into a bottle, shaking well to mix. Add the water and shake again.

After-sun balm

The ability of lavender to soothe and heal burns was discovered early this century. Combined with chamomile, this cream makes an efficacious remedy for sunburn.

4½ tbsp (65 ml) unscented
moisturizing body lotion
20 drops chamomile essential oil
30 drops lavender essential oil

Decant the moisturizing lotion into a bowl and mix in the oils very thoroughly. Bottle and use after sunbathing to soothe your skin.

Scented water like this Florida water (above) looks wonderful in an antique bottle and is ideal as a cooling splash on hot summer days. The soothing and healing after-sun balm (left) uses an unperfumed moisturizing lotion as its base with the addition of lavender and chamomile essential oils.

autumn

Today I think
Only with scents – scents dead leaves yield,
And bracken, and wild carrot's seed,
  And the square mustard field.

Odours that rise
When the spade wounds the root of the tree,
Rose, currant, raspberry or goutweed,
Rhubarb or celery:

The smoke's smell, too,
    Flowing from where a bonfire burns
    The dead, the waste, the dangerous,
      And all to sweetness turns . . .

ALL TO SWEETNESS TURNS
Edward Thomas (1878–1917)

As the year progresses, a day always comes when my focus turns from outdoors to indoors and then I know that autumn is on its way. The trees may still be covered in green leaves and the days hot and sunny, but the autumnal fragrances are in the air – the evening chill that sets the nose twitching, a rich ripeness to fruit and foliage, and heavy morning dews that weigh down the late summer blooms and release their spicy scents. I look forward to cosy evenings around the fire, rooms fragrant with beeswax polish and potpourri and warming meals, rich with herbs and spices. Harvesting, preserving and storing are deeply satisfying autumn activities and while they are no longer essential to our survival, they keep us in contact with the circle of the seasons and acknowledge our deeper instincts.

There is a pungency to the blooms of autumn that is as intense as the hues of the flowers. The characteristically spicy scent of deep bronze and gold chrysanthemums, the peppery aroma of vibrant scarlet and gold nasturtiums (a colloquial French name actually means "nose twister") and the musky fragrance of late phlox, combine with the smell of fallen leaves and damp air to create an earthy aroma that could belong to no other time.

Not all the plants in the autumn garden are well-scented, but they are desirable nonetheless – the fuchsia, the Japanese anemone, the Michaelmas daisy – all give color and form, but for extra scent I rely on the plants of late summer which continue flowering until the first frosts: salvias, *Cosmos atrosanguineus* (the deliciously chocolate-scented

Now is the time for the burning of the leaves.
They go to the fire; the nostril pricks with smoke
Wandering slowly into a seeping mist . . .

They will come again, the leaf and the flower, to arise
From squalor of rottenness into the old splendour,
And magical scents to a wondering memory bring;
The same glory, to shine upon different eyes.
Earth cares for her own ruins, naught for ours.
Nothing is certain, only the certain spring.

THE BURNING OF THE LEAVES
Laurence Binyon (1869–1943)

Autumn is filled with pungent, fruity fragrances, smoky bonfires and misty mornings. It is also a season of rich colors: the bronze blooms of the chrysanthemum, the ruby red of the rose hip and the golden yellow of the pumpkin.

cosmos), verbenas and roses. Plants that were cut back after their first flowering may flower again in late summer and early autumn.

Now is the time for a final gathering of aromatic bunches of thyme, sage and marjoram to dry for winter use. It is also prudent to provide winter protection for tender plants such as tarragon and lemon thyme, and bring lemon verbena and rosemary indoors.

An antique Victorian cloche is the perfect winter home for a selection of potted herbs in my mild-winter area. Placed in a sheltered position near the kitchen door, it ensures that I have fresh flavors even when the herb bed is under snow.

Pots of herbs

Although I have used an antique cloche, you can keep your herbs equally well in a modern cloche, cold frame or greenhouse; anywhere in fact that will give the herbs some protection against frost and stop them getting cold and wet. You can use a proprietary potting mixture, but I find that the herbs do better in a mix that contains both peat and loam with added grit, so I make up a bag for this purpose.

Herbs in decorative pots with handwritten labels are always welcome presents for someone without a garden; chives and parsley are both very happy on the windowsill.

Your favorite herbs – I have chosen curly and flat-leafed parsley, sage, rosemary, lemon thyme and chives

Terracotta or plastic pots

Potting mixture – 2 parts loam, 2 parts peat-based (or peat substitute) and 1 part coarse grit

Broken pieces of pottery (for terracotta)

Gift tags, optional

Remove the herbs from their existing pots and tease loose the root ball; this will help the plants establish in the new potting mixture.

If you are using terracotta pots, place some broken pottery in the bottom to aid drainage. Place the plants in the pots, firming in around the roots with potting mixture, pressing down as you work to prevent any air spaces. Water thoroughly before placing in a cloche, greenhouse or cold frame. Then water sparingly.

Herbs are not the only plants that require attention. Pots of tender plants such as citrus, *Datura* and geraniums should be moved into the house or greenhouse as soon as there is a danger of frost.

Specially formulated winter feeds are now available to keep citrus trees in good condition over the winter, although I have found that a certain amount of benign neglect is better for them than constant attention.

It is possible to buy modern copies of this wonderful Victorian cloche, but your potted herbs will be just as useful even if they are over-wintered in more modest surroundings. Pot up some extras to give to friends.

Winter pansy trough

Winter-flowering pansies are at their most glorious in the autumn, and provided they are regularly deadheaded they will keep on flowering throughout the winter in mild-winter areas (Zone 7b and warmer) and enjoy another flush of flowers in the spring. Their scent is faint but distinct, and by underplanting them with miniature narcissus you are guaranteed a long-lasting display with the added bonus of fragrance in the spring.

This makes a good gift to take when visiting friends or relatives for a weekend – a (hopefully) pleasant reminder of your visit long after you have returned home. Add an attractive, hand-written tag or garden label giving instructions for watering and dead-heading the plants.

Decorative trough
Potting mixture
20 'Tête-à-Tête' narcissus bulbs
6–8 winter-flowering pansies
Garden label or gift tag, optional

Half fill the trough with potting mixture. Push the narcissus bulbs firmly into the potting mixture. Carefully tap and squeeze the pots to remove the pansies and place them evenly across the trough. Fill any spaces between the plants with more potting mixture, firming in the plants with your fingers as you work.

Water thoroughly and stand in a sunny position. Water in dry weather and deadhead the pansies regularly.

The secret of success with winter pansies is to deadhead them regularly. Underplanted with narcissus they will be even more glorious in the spring. Plant one for yourself and one for a friend.

Épices de Provence
Provençal Spices

Most of my herbs and spices are stored separately, so that I can blend them when needed, but there is one spice mix that takes a bit of preparation, so I make up a large batch ready for instant use. The *Epices de Provence* is a traditional aromatic blend from the south of France and delicious in the richly flavored dishes of the region. It is quite pungent, so use it sparingly.

As ideal presents for gourmet cooks, make up small fabric bags in pretty Provençal prints and place clear packets of the spice mix inside. Tie with a bright ribbon and attach a descriptive label giving some recipe ideas.

A rich and satisfying spice mix, Epices de Provence *can be bottled or packaged as an unusual and practical present. Make sure you add a label giving ingredients used in the blend and perhaps a recipe suggestion, too.*

AUTUMN HERBS are gathered from the garden on a fine day early in the season, when the dew has evaporated, but before midday, so that the herbs will retain the maximum concentration of volatile oils. They are then bundled up and tied with garden twine. If the crop is sufficiently large I will probably leave some hanging as decorative bunches in the kitchen, but the herbs that I plan to use for cooking are wrapped in cones of brown paper before being suspended from the drying rack. This keeps the color strong and prevents any dust settling on the leaves. If your kitchen is as warm as mine, two weeks' drying time will be ample. The herbs are then removed from their paper cones and the leaves are stripped from the stems. Store in airtight jars or tins and keep in a dark cupboard.

As I open the door of my spice cupboard I am enveloped in a gloriously aromatic fragrance, a combination of the many exotic spices that will add scent and savor to our meals. Slow-cooked stews and casseroles, flavored with garlic and herbs; spicy cakes and puddings – these are the flavors and fragrances of the season.

2 oz (50 g) thyme
1 oz (25 g) savory
1 oz (25 g) lavender flowers
1 oz (25 g) rosemary
1 oz (25 g) bay leaves
1 oz (25 g) cloves
1 oz (25 g) dried orange peel
1 whole nutmeg, grated
Makes 7 oz (200 g)

Although the herbs and spices are traditionally ground together in a mortar and pestle, I have found that the quickest way to achieve the fine blend required is first to process all the ingredients in a blender and then to complete the process in an electric coffee grinder. The mixture can then be stored in airtight containers and stowed away in the spice cupboard.

CHILI (Capsicum) has been grown in central and south America since pre-Hispanic times. In 1493, Columbus brought it to Europe, and although we assume that it has always been part of the Asian diet, it was in fact unknown there until the Portuguese introduced it in the 16th century. India is now the largest producer, growing 80,000 tons of chilis a year.

Chilis are part of the *Capsicum* family, which includes the sweet pepper, and there is an enormous variation in hotness, according to the amount of capsaicin (the hot agent) contained in the plant. Cayenne pepper is made from ground *Capsicum minimum* and C. *frutescens*, while chili powder is generally made from a blend of different chilis. Contrary to popular opinion, red chilis are not hotter than green ones, they are simply riper and because they are sweeter, their flavor is different.

When I handle chilis, I always wear thin rubber gloves, as even careful handling seems to cause some skin irritation. It is essential that you never touch your face – and especially your eyes – when handling chilis as it can be a most painful experience. If eating chili dishes proves to be an uncomfortable experience, drink beer or spirits: capsaicin is soluble in alcohol, so an alcoholic drink works as an antidote.

A chili-flavored oil is a perfect present to take to a barbecue, as it can be put to immediate use on grilled meats or vegetables. Attractive glass bottles are available to buy quite inexpensively in kitchenware shops; or recycle ones that previously contained olive or other oils.

GARLIC (Allium sativum) is of such antiquity that its origins are uncertain. It was generally believed to have originated in southern Siberia, although this may not be entirely accurate as an expedition to Afghanistan in the 1960s discovered an unknown variety growing there. Whatever its botanical origins, there is no doubt that it has been considered a herb of the utmost importance throughout history. The Greeks and Romans consumed vast quantities, although even then – because of its disinctive aroma – it had its detractors. Horace is recorded to have considered the consumption of it a sign of vulgarity, a prejudice which was even recorded in Mrs. Grieve's *A Modern Herbal* (published in 1931), in which she states that "in the southern countries of Europe it is a common ingredient in dishes, and is largely consumed by the agricultural population."

In medieval gardens, the "gar leek" (old English for spear leek – from its leaf shape) was a crop of great importance both for its health-giving properties and its ability to make the food of the day more palatable; and it certainly wasn't grown only by the peasants. The gardens of Glastonbury Abbey were full of garlic to supply the abbey and the manor. In 1333 there is a record of 11,000 garlic cloves in store.

The healing properties of garlic have long been recognized and much that was previously ascribed to superstition has been found to be medically correct; for example, regular consumption of garlic is good for the heart. Undoubtedly, much of the prejudice against it must have been due to its

aroma. During the First World War, diluted garlic juice, was used on dressings to prevent wounds becoming infected. It is reported that the treatment was very successful, as the garlic proved to be a powerful antiseptic. Nowadays, those who wish to use garlic medicinally can do so in an odorless form, leaving the delicious aroma to have nothing but pleasant culinary associations.

In our family, we use huge quantities of garlic. My children are partial to whole garlic cloves roasted in their skins along with the roast potatoes that we have for Sunday lunch; but even when less obvious, there are few savory dishes that leave my kitchen without the inclusion of garlic.

Confit of garlic

When I am able to obtain a large quantity of really first-class garlic, I like to make up some confit of garlic. The garlic is gently poached in good olive oil and becomes wonderfully mellow and is delicious spread on crusty bread. I also use the confit in subtle dishes more suited to a hint of garlic than a kick. If you have some oil left over when you bottle the confit; keep this in a separate bottle for brushing on grilled meats and vegetables or for frying. Keep the confit in the refrigerator and use within two weeks.

Make up several jars and decorate some with plaited raffia and heads of garlic to present to gourmet friends as a really unusual gift.

4 oz (100 g) of peeled garlic cloves
1 cup (250 ml) of olive oil
Sterilized jars with tight-fitting seals
Gift packaging, optional
Makes one 1 lb (450 g) jar

Capture the fabulous flavor of garlic in this rich and mellow confit. Make enough jars so that others can share this wonderful experience.

Place garlic in a saucepan and cover with the oil. Bring to a simmer and cook over a moderate to low heat for 20–25 minutes or until the garlic is tender. Cool and store in the refrigerator for up to 1 week; or freeze.

Chili and garlic oil

This is a recipe of my own, devised to give a mellower taste and to avoid the problems caused by putting fresh herbs and flavorings into oils and vinegars.

4–5 yellow Thai chilis
5 large peeled garlic cloves
1 tsp black peppercorns
1¼ cups (300 ml) light olive oil
Makes approximately 1½ cups (350 ml)

Roast the chilis and garlic in a hot oven for 10 minutes until lightly colored, then place them in a suitable bottle with the peppercorns. Fill to the brim with olive oil and cork tightly.

Store in the refrigerator for up to 1 week; or freeze.

Pizza oil

I first encountered pizza oil in the pizzerias of Nice, where pizzas cooked in wood-fired ovens are the best I've ever tasted, and every table has a bottle of aromatic oil.

1 tbsp mixed peppercorns
Generous sprig of fresh thyme
Generous sprig of fresh rosemary
4 dried red chilis (2 crushed)
3 roasted garlic cloves
2 cups (500 ml) virgin olive oil
Makes 2¼ cups (550 ml)

Place all the flavorings in a suitable bottle and pour on the oil. Cork and refrigerate for up to one week. To store for longer periods, strain out the herbs and spices and freeze oil.

The pizza oil (left) will enhance the blandest pizza, while the chili and garlic oil (right) is subtly spicy.

GINGER *(Zingiber officinale)*, in its powdered form, was a favorite spice of the Romans, who appear to have introduced it into Europe from Africa. Its use remained widespread in the Middle Ages when ginger and saffron seemed to be essential flavorings in a huge number of dishes. The plant was taken to the New World by the Spanish and it became naturalized in America and the West Indies. Jamaican powdered ginger developed the reputation of being the very finest, a reputation which it still holds to this day. By the 18th century, the extensive use of fruits and spices in meat dishes had largely died out and powdered ginger became a spice primarily for puddings, cakes and biscuits.

Until a few years ago, fresh root ginger was a rare commodity and only available from specialist shops. Now, I am pleased to say, it graces the shelves of almost every supermarket and its use seems nearly as ubiquitous as powdered ginger was in the 15th century.

If, like me, you find the lusciously plump piece of ginger you bought and used once, too frequently transforms itself into a sad, shrunken root in the salad drawer of the refrigerator, you may like to follow cookery doyenne Elizabeth David's two recommendations for keeping it in good condition. First, it freezes well, so cut a large root into smaller pieces and keep them in a bag in the freezer ready for use; or secondly, peel the ginger, place it in a jar covered with dry sherry and store in the refrigerator. Either way you will always have fresh ginger on hand.

CINNAMON *(Cinnamomum zeylanicum)* has a history so colorful that it is worth repeating here. When the Arabs first brought spices to the Ancient Greeks, they ensured that the trade remained firmly in their hands by telling wild tales of the origins of these exotic flavorings. Herodotus recorded their account of the cinnamon harvest: "... the dry sticks are brought by large birds which carry them to their nests ... on mountain precipices which no man can climb, and that the method that the Arabians have invented for getting hold of them is to cut up the bodies of dead oxen, or donkeys, or other animals, into very large joints which they carry to the spot in question and leave on the ground near the nests. They then retire to a safe distance and the birds fly down and carry off the joints of meat to their nests, which not being strong enough to bear the weight, break and fall to the ground. Then the men come along and pick up the cinnamon ...."

The reality is more prosaic. The cinnamon tree is a member of the Laurel Family and a native of Ceylon. Historically, as with many other spices,

the Dutch held the monopoly on harvesting wild cinnamon and, in the belief that it might lose its aromatic properties and to protect a profitable trade, they did not allow its cultivation until 1776. Their fears that cultivation would denature the cinnamon proved unfounded and it is now cultivated widely in Ceylon and southern India.

The cinnamon sticks are actually the dried, inner bark of young shoots from coppiced trees. Every two years, the cinnamon is harvested during the rainy season, when it peels away easily from the stems. The outer bark is removed and as the inner bark dries, it naturally curls up to make the "cigars" with which we are familiar.

The aromatic quality of cinnamon is variable and, once powdered, it will begin to deteriorate. As a general rule, the fresher the cinnamon, the less you'll need.

These days cinnamon sticks are as popular with florists and decorators as they are with cooks. Bunched together and tied with a generous raffia bow they look highly decorative piled high in an old pottery bowl. As the scent of cinnamon sticks is only really released when they are crushed, it is a good idea to put a few drops of cinnamon oil on swabs of cotton wool and tuck these in among your decorations to enhance the aroma.

Medicinally, cinnamon has long been a popular cure for colds and sore throats.

This spiced apple cake would make an ideal gift to take to your hosts for a country weekend full of fresh air and exercise.

Spiced apple cake

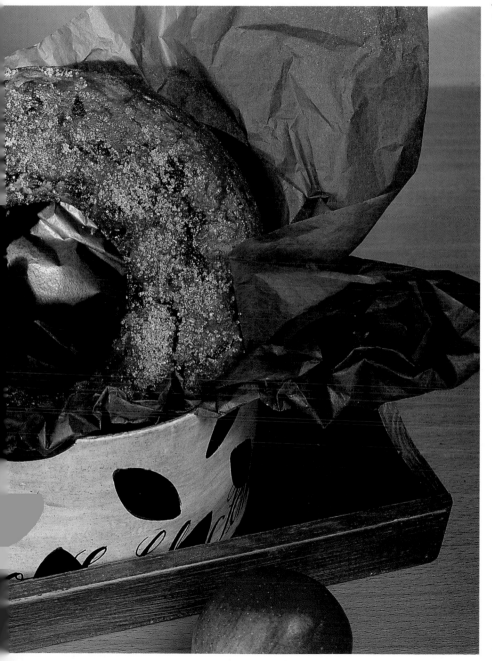

One of my family's autumn favorites is spiced apple cake.

Once baked and cooled, pack into a pretty tin and tie with a wide satin ribbon as a thank you gift when visiting friends for the weekend.

1 cup (225 g) applesauce

½ cup (100 g) unsalted butter

1 cup (200 g) demerara sugar

2 eggs

2½ cups (275 g) flour
(half whole wheat/half white)

2 tsp baking powder

¾ cup (150 g) raisins

¾ cup (150 g) sultanas

1 cup (100 g) walnuts (chopped)

½ tsp salt

½ tsp cloves

1 tsp cinnamon

½ tsp nutmeg

8 in (20 cm) ring pan

Beat the butter and sugar until light and creamy, add the eggs gradually one at a time. Sift together the flour, spices and baking powder. Toss the fruit and nuts in 1 tbsp of flour. Gradually add the flour mixture and applesauce alternately to the sugar/butter/egg mix. Finally fold in the dried fruit and nuts.

Pour into the greased baking pan and bake at 350°F/180°C for 40 minutes or until a skewer comes out clean from the cake. Leave to cool for 15 minutes before removing from pan.

JUNIPER *(Juniperus)* was used by the Ancient Egyptians for medicinal and cosmetic purposes. Medicinally, it was used to alleviate asthma, and when combined with frankincense it was a popular headache cure, while cosmetically it was a central ingredient of black hair dye.

In Europe in the Middle Ages, it was valued for its fumigant properties, and branches were burned to protect against the plague and other infectious diseases. In 19th-century Paris, it was burned during smallpox epidemics and even earlier this century, French hospitals burned juniper berries. Its aromatic qualities have been appreciated for centuries, and many blends of potpourri have included juniper berries.

The volatile oil from juniper berries is the main flavoring of Hollands or Geneva gin, which gets its name from the French for juniper, *genévrier*.

Apple and other fruit jellies are particularly delicious with the addition of herbs and spices. Juniper jelly is flavored with gin as well as juniper berries to make a fragrant accompaniment to game.

Juniper jelly

In cookery, the juniper berry is an important flavoring in pâtés and terrines and is often used when cooking game, where its flavor and aroma is strong enough to compete with the highly flavored meats. Juniper-flavored apple jelly is a delicious accompaniment to game or pork.

For anyone with apple trees in the garden, making a selection of differently flavored apple jellies will help deal with the autumn glut. Alternatively, wild or cultivated crab apples make a deliciously rich jelly.

To make attractive presents, pot up the jelly in glass jars and mark out circles on to pretty, printed fabrics, about 1½ in (4 cm) larger than the lids of the jars. Cut round with pinking shears or scissors and fix to the lid with a rubber band and piece of decorative ribbon or twine. Add a handwritten label, cut in the shape of an apple.

2 lb (1 kg) cooking apples
2½ cups (600 ml) water
2 oz (60 g) lightly crushed juniper berries
Small muslin square
Jelly bag
Preserving sugar
2 drops juniper essential oil
1 tbsp gin
Sterilized jars, seals and lids
Fabric, labels, etc, optional

Chop the apples roughly, including the core and the skin, and place in a large pan with the water. Tie the juniper berries in the muslin and add to the pan. Simmer until soft, then place in the jelly bag and allow to drain.

For each 1 pint (600 ml) of juice allow 1 lb (500 g) of sugar. Return the juice to the pan, add the sugar. Boil rapidly until the jelly reaches setting point. Add the juniper oil and gin.

Autumn treat

I have used a pumpkin as a container for this autumnal arrangement of leaves, berries and flowers. The pungent fragrance of chrysanthemums combines with the scents of lavender leaves and autumn fruits to make this an aromatic as well as a visual feast.

If you plan to give this arrangement as a present, ask at the produce department of your supermarket for a shallow wooden vegetable tray, line it with fresh moss and stand your display in the center.

Large pumpkin

3–4 blocks of green florists' foam

Sprays of autumn fruits (blackberries, crab apples, japonica, rose hips and blackthorn)

Fern fronds

5–7 large chrysanthemums

Lavender foliage

Florists' wire

Selection of fruit: apples, quinces, pomegranates, crabapples

Use a knife to remove the top from the pumpkin, remove the seeds and most of the flesh, but be careful not to puncture the skin.

Soak the florists' foam in water and cut it to to fit into the "pumpkin bowl."

Create the outline of the arrangement with various sprays of fruit, berries and fern fronds. Don't make it too symmetrical – nature isn't. Add the chrysanthemums and lavender. Finally, wire the fruit and add it to the display, packing each piece close together for a lavish effect.

You don't need to be a great artist to create the rich colors and opulence of this display. A hollowed-out pumpkin holds a glorious collection of fine autumn fruits and flowers. Use the flesh of the pumpkin in a pie or serve with roast meat and vegetables in a spicy bake.

Aromatic lavender

One of the consolations of being confined indoors as the autumn wind and rain lash against the windows, is the opportunity to work on dried flower arrangements made with the new season's crop. "Fresh dried flowers" may sound like a contradiction in terms, but the recently harvested and dried flowers are infinitely superior in color and fragrance to those that were picked the previous year.

In my work as a dried flower designer, I use huge quantities of lavender, far more than I can grow myself, so I buy the majority from a company that imports French lavender from Provence. Opening a new box of lavender is a deeply aromatic experience, a transport of delight that has me dreaming of the rich purple lavender fields of the Drôme in the baking heat of the summer sun.

I love the sculptural look of these arrangements. Terracotta pots are the perfect containers for the sheaves of lavender, and a matching pair of pots look marvellous either side of a fireplace. The secret of success with arranging lavender is to be really generous with the quantity; it needs to be densely packed to create the right effect.

For a special wedding gift, adapt this design to make an ornamental lavender urn.

Terracotta pots
Dry florists' foam
20–24 bunches of lavender
Spanish moss

Cut foam so that it fits into pots and end just below lip. Take 10–15 stems of lavender at a time, hold them loosely in your hand with heads resting on work surface so that they are level. Trim stems to the same length and insert bundle into foam, starting at center of pot.

Repeat this process, working towards the outside of the pot and gradually sloping the lavender so that you create a gently curved outline. Fill the pot right to the edge with lavender and tuck moss at the base to ensure that no foam is visible.

There is little to beat the intense and heady fragrance of dried lavender. Formal arrangements, such as these, are much in demand and would thrill any recipient lucky enough to receive one.

SCENTED CANDLES, at their very simplest, can be made by dripping some essential oil into melted wax around the wick of a burning candle. Be careful not to put the oil on to the flame itself, or it will burn off instantly. Not all essential oils are suitable for burning in this way and some can even smell quite unpleasant, so it is important to test your fragrance in the way described above before making your own scented candles.

Seasonal scented candles make good gifts either individually or together. As well as the autumn blend of sandalwood, cedar and lime (page 92), the winter blend could include the Christmas oils of mandarin and cinnamon, while spring evokes fresh scents such as lemon, lavender and geranium, and the summer candle, if scented with citronella, can be used in the evening garden to ward off mosquitos and other bugs.

Individual pastry tins can be used as molds for scented floating candles. You will need to use special wicks which are available for this purpose. Float the candles in a glass bowl with flowers and fruit for a table centerpiece.

Floating lights

Although special molds are available to make floating candles, I like to use individual metal pastry tins as they are slightly larger and easier to obtain. Scent them according to your mood. Fresh lemony scents for an alfresco meal or spicy, woody oils for a cosy winter dinner.

6 oz (175 g) paraffin wax

6 in (15 cm) floating candle wicks (available from specialist suppliers)

6 small metal pastry tins

30 drops of your chosen essential oil

Melt the wax in a double boiler. Pour carefully into the molds to avoid air bubbles. Leave until half set and then cut the wicks into 1 in (2.5 cm) lengths and insert into the still soft wax. Leave to set fully and unmold.

Scented flowerpot candles

Two 3 in (8 cm) diameter clay flowerpots, preferably old

Small piece of self-hardening clay to plug the holes in the bottom of the pots

Two 6 in (15 cm) lengths of 2–4 in (5–10 cm) wick (ideally slow-burning metal core wick which is available from specialist suppliers)

2 oz (50 g) natural beeswax

Double boiler

6 oz (175 g) paraffin wax

20 drops sandalwood essential oil

20 drops cedarwood essential oil

10 drops lime essential oil

Glass or terracotta pots are ideal containers for fragrant candles. These are quite expensive to buy, but cost much less to make, especially if you raid the garden shed for lovely old pots.

I love the look of candles made in old flowerpots and as this method uses the simplest technique, it's the one I employ when making scented candles. Experiment with the fragrances you use, a single oil can be just as good and sometimes better than a blend, especially when you are just beginning. As this is an autumnal project, I have used the woody fragrances of sandalwood and cedar with fruity lime. Remember that these oils are much subtler than synthetic fragrances and that the aroma the candles diffuse will be quite gentle.

It is essential to use a double boiler or a heatproof bowl over a pan of water as wax is highly flammable.

Plug the base of the pots with the clay and leave to harden. Position the wick centrally in the pot, keeping it in place by attaching it to a stick laid across the top of the pot.

Melt the beeswax in the double boiler (or a heatproof bowl over a pan of boiling water) and then add the paraffin wax. Remove from the heat as soon as it has melted. Allow to cool slightly and then add the essential oils. Stir thoroughly.

Pour the wax into the pots; do this gently to avoid air bubbles. (Reserve a small amount of wax in the double boiler.) Fill the pots to within ¼ in (6 mm) of the rim.

As the wax cools a hollow will form around the wick; use a needle to break the surface tension and pour more wax into the hollow.

Once the candle is cool, trim the wick and prime it with a little wax so that it will light readily and burn brightly.

Rolled beeswax candle

It is hard to beat the fragrance and appearance of a candle rolled from a sheet of honeycomb beeswax and, as the technique is very easy, even a complete beginner will achieve creditable results.

1 sheet of beeswax, 8 × 13½ in
(20 × 35 cm)

10 in (25 cm) length of wick suitable for
beeswax candles

Makes 1 candle

The wax should be at room temperature. To test that it is ready, press the wax with your finger, you should be able to press it easily. If the wax is too cold, warm it with a hairdryer.

Lay the wick along the left-hand side of the sheet and carefully roll the sheet as tightly as possible from left to right, being careful to keep the base straight. Once you have completed the process, gently press the edges to prevent it unrolling. Trim the wick to ½ in (12 mm) long and rub it with beeswax to ensure it will light.

Making rolled beeswax candles couldn't be simpler and I have yet to meet anyone who wasn't absolutely delighted to receive some. A bundle of candles tied with black satin ribbon looks very sophisticated and makes an ideal gift.

Woodland potpourri

In our house, at this time of year, piles of brilliantly colored leaves and glossy nuts are trophies brought home from woodland walks to be arranged into a still life. Although beautiful, these treasures do not last long. Instead, capture the fragrance and memories of autumn walks with this woodland potpourri, which is a mixture of barks, cones, berries, leaves and spices with a distinctly autumnal look and scent.

The oils used are spicy and resinous, making this a fragrant gift which will appeal to men. Why not fill a Shaker-style box with this autumnal potpourri, secure with sisal string, and add a parcel label to make a suitably masculine gift?

You may find that some of the ingredients, like alder cones and rosehips, can be gathered from your own garden, but if you have difficulty in obtaining any items, you can always substitute other cones, seeds or pods. Although some, like the star anise, have a distinct fragrance, it is primarily the orris root powder and the oils that give the potpourri its fragrance, so don't be afraid to experiment with the other ingredients.

— the season of smoky bonfires, brilliant rustling leaves that settle into soft muted decay, of sooty wet walnuts, freshly polished chestnuts and musty wild mushrooms.

1 oz (25 g) coriander seeds
1 oz (25 g) juniper berries
Mortar and pestle
1 oz (25 g) orris root powder
10 drops cedarwood essential oil
8 drops sandalwood essential oil
5 drops patchouli essential oil
5 drops bergamot essential oil
1 drop clove essential oil
Rubber gloves
2 oz (50 g) alder cones
4 oz (100 g) hops
1 oz (25 g) buckthorn bark or cinnamon sticks
1 oz (25 g) whole star anise
1 oz (25 g) golden mushrooms
4 oz (100 g) rose hips/bay berries
Lidded bowl or glass jar

Place the coriander seeds and juniper berries in a mortar and crush lightly with the pestle to release their fragrance. Add the orris root powder and all the essential oils and work into a dryish paste, wearing the rubber gloves to protect your hands.

Place the remaining ingredients and the essential oil mixture in a large glass or china bowl and mix thoroughly.

Store the potpourri mixture in a large lidded bowl or glass jar. Leave to cure for six weeks, shaking the mix every few days. When ready, display the potpourri in a shallow, polished wooden bowl or box, or package as a gift.

Hop flowers introduce color as well as their distinctive aroma to this autumnal potpourri mix. A large wooden bowl provides a perfect setting and invites you to dip your hands in to release yet more fragrance. Give some to a deskbound executive to remind him or her of the world outside.

Eau de Cologne

An Italian barber who went to seek his fortune in Germany first marketed his *Aqua Admirabilis* under the name of Eau de Cologne in 1709. This "water" was made with rectified grape spirit and oils of neroli, bergamot, lavender and rosemary. It was hugely popular in Cologne, both for its fragrance and as a panacea for many ills including skin, stomach and gum complaints, and was even used for veterinary purposes.

With essential oils now readily available, it is extremely simple to make your own cologne and to experiment with your own formulations once you have tried the process. Eau de Cologne is a refreshing "splash" fragrance, especially if you keep it in the refrigerator. If the scent is too strong, it can be diluted with more bottled water.

A decorative glass bottle filled with home-made Eau de Cologne is a pleasantly nostalgic gift for an elderly friend or relative.

½ cup (100 ml) of 100 percent proof vodka
Sterilized wide-necked screw-top jar
20 drops orange essential oil
10 drops bergamot essential oil
10 drops lemon essential oil
2 drops rosemary essential oil
2 drops neroli essential oil
¼ cup (50 ml) still bottled water
Paper filter
¾ cup (150 ml) colored glass bottle, sterilized

Pour the vodka into the wide-necked jar and add the essential oils, stirring gently but thoroughly to ensure a good mix. Leave to stand for 48 hours.

Add the still bottled water, again stirring gently but thoroughly. Leave the liquid to stand for at least another 48 hours, but ideally for four to six weeks so the cologne can develop its full strength and maturity.

Strain through a paper filter and decant into the bottle. Label clearly.

Eau de Cologne has remained enduringly popular since 1709 as it is equally suitable for men and women. While the original recipe is the carefully guarded property of Roger & Gallet, this version makes a most acceptable gift.

Scented linen bags

One of the small domestic dreams that I aspire to is a perfectly ordered linen cupboard. Given that this dream is unlikely to become reality, I at least make up for the lack of order by ensuring that my linen cupboard smells wonderful, with scented bags tucked among the sheets.

Antique linen or cotton pillowcases can sometimes be bought quite inexpensively. Tie a pair together with a pretty ribbon and attach a scented linen bag to make a really special gift.

2 oz (50 g) dried rose petals

½ oz (15 g) shredded oakmoss

1 oz (25 g) whole cloves

1 tbsp powdered cinnamon

1tbsp powdered allspice

1 tbsp dried rosemary

1 tonquin bean

2 star anise

5 drops bergamot essential oil

5 drops lavender essential oil

Screw-top jar

8 cotton bags, 3 × 6 in (8 × 15 cm)

Ribbon

Makes 8 bags

Measure out the rose petals, oakmoss and cloves into a bowl. Place the cinnamon and allspice in a smaller bowl. Coarsely crush the rosemary, tonquin bean and star anise in a mortar and pestle and add to the cinnamon and allspice.

Add the oils to the spices, working them in well. Mix the spices with the rose petals, oakmoss and cloves. Store in a screw-top jar for one month to allow the mix to mature.

When the mixture is ready, divide it between the eight bags and tie with ribbon.

Brightly colored fabric bags hold a deliciously aromatic mix of rose petals, oakmoss and essential oils which will impart a rich scent.

Southernwood moth sachets

These moth bags combine southernwood with tansy, oakmoss, cinnamon and cloves to make a really practical present. They look and smell wonderful – a feast for the eye that will curtail a feast for the moths!

In the old Herbals, the ability of plants to repel insects was of prime importance and none was rated higher in this quality than southernwood. Its French name *garde-robe* reflects that it has long been the chosen remedy against moth attack on garments which have been stored away.

These sachets combine southernwood with other aromatic herbs to make a fragrant repellent; use at least two to a drawer or four to a closet.

When giving a knitted present, enclose it in a zipped sweater bag complete with its own southernwood moth bag.

2 oz (50 g) southernwood
1 oz (25 g) tansy
1 oz (25 g) powdered orris root
1 oz (25 g) shredded oakmoss
½ oz (15 g) whole cloves
2 cinnamon sticks, broken into small pieces
6 finely woven cotton bags, 3 × 6 in (8 × 15 cm)
Ribbon
Gift packaging, optional
Makes 6 bags

Mix all the ingredients together thoroughly in a large bowl. Store in a sealed container for two weeks to allow the mix to mature, then divide between the cotton bags and tie with a length of ribbon. Use as needed or pack up as a gift in a little wicker hamper, decorative tin, or with a piece of knitwear, as described above.

Massage oils

Essential oils can be used for health, beauty, relaxation, to scent the home and even in cooking. All are pleasurable, but the most enjoyable of all is an aromatherapy massage, especially when the oils have been blended to match your mood.

As a writer I spend a lot of time sitting at a desk using my brain too much and my body too little. I do exercise regularly, sometimes reluctantly, but I have no mixed feelings about my weekly aromatherapy massage, which I no longer regard as self-indulgence or a luxury, but rather as an essential part of keeping fit and well.

As its name suggests, aromatherapy is therapeutic as well as pleasurable and relaxing, and a skilled aromatherapist will assess your mood, fitness and needs and use a blend of oils that will be specially chosen for you on each occasion.

When you are using essential oils at home, it is important to follow guidelines on which oils can be used safely. If you are pregnant or have a medical condition, such as high blood pressure, certain oils should be avoided, make sure that you follow the directions, particularly about diluting essential oils, carefully. These oils are highly concentrated and can cause skin irritations and have other adverse effects when used incorrectly.

The two recipes given here use oils that are considered safe, but if you have an existing medical condition, you should check with your doctor before using aromatherapy. When using massage oils on children or babies, dilute the oils with 100 percent more sweet almond oil.

Give your partner a bottle of each oil as a birthday or anniversary present – a present you can really share.

RELAXING OIL
¼ cup (50 ml) sweet almond oil
15 drops lavender essential oil
10 drops chamomile essential oil

Add the essential oils to the bottle of almond oil and shake well to blend. Label clearly.

STIMULATING OIL
¼ cup (50 ml) sweet almond oil
15 drops geranium essential oil
10 drops bergamot essential oil

Add the essential oils to the bottle of almond oil and shake well to blend. Label clearly.

Do not use this oil when sunbathing, as bergamot can cause skin discoloration.

winter

The green pine-needles shiver glassily,
 Each cased in ice. Harsh winter, grey and dun,
 Shuts out the sun.
But with live, scarlet fire,
 Enfolding seed of sweet Junes yet to be,
 Rose-berries melt the snow, and burn above
The thorny briar,
Like beauty with its deathless seed of love.

ROSE-BERRIES
Mary Webb (1881–1927)

The long, dark days of winter have always been a time for festivals, a time to raise the spirits and look forward to the coming year. Many of the ceremonies that we now associate with Christmas long pre-date Christianity and grew from a combination of Druid superstition, Roman Saturnalia, and Norse candlelight ceremonies.

As someone who grew up far away from England, I always longed for a traditional English Christmas – the house decked with aromatic pine, holly and ivy, the tables groaning with spiced festive fare, a blazing yule log, and *marrons glacés*. The last item was the result of reading too many Victorian and Edwardian novels in which a taste for *marrons glacés* was portrayed as the height of sophistication.

Each year, I teach a series of Christmas workshops at the Chelsea Physic Garden in London, in which I pass on my tips for the best possible Christmas with the least possible effort. Most of us fall into the trap of trying to get it all perfect and end up either exhausted and resentful or feeling that we have failed. These workshops are designed to suggest a fresh approach which, at its most basic, can memorably be described as "The Slut's Christmas" – light the candles, switch out the lights, polish the taps and mull some wine! In other words, if you create the right atmosphere, the rest becomes secondary. As a "cured" perfectionist I can recommend this approach to life in general; a lot more relaxing and much more fun.

Like most gardeners, I tend to take the view that winter is the time to browse through seed cata-

logues, read gardening books and dream of what's to come, with just the occasional foray outside when the sun is shining. In mild winter areas, you do not need to be a dedicated all-weather winter gardener to benefit from these plants, if you plant them next to frequently used paths, beside doorways and in pots and tubs on a deck or windowsill where you can enjoy them without getting muddy feet.

The fragile beauty and the haunting perfume of

Dried orange slices threaded with gold cord and gilded leaves adorn jars of seasonal, spicy mincemeat – traditional fare for this time of year.

winter flowers are doubly precious for the unexpectedness of their flowering when all around is dull and drear. This is nature at its most extraordinary when among the pallid browns and grays sudden flashes of color catch the eye and fragrance is wafted on the sun-warmed breeze. These flowers are soloists, confident to take the stage alone, rather than join the massed ranks of summer and I recommend that at least some are invited to perform in every mild-climate winter garden.

Many of the plants that flower in winter can be quite dull at other times of the year, so they are best planted among other plants which will provide interest while they are resting. There are a number of winter-flowering shrubs that are worth considering. One of my favorites is the witch hazel (*Hamamelis mollis*). In the middle of winter (in USDA hardiness Zone 6 and warmer), its bare branches are covered with piercingly fragrant yellow flowers which emerge directly from the branches and have been described as looking like sea-anemones. The best varieties are *H. mollis pallida* and *H. vernalis* 'Sandra'. Not all *Hamamelis* are scented so it is important to buy a named scented variety.

Choose a sheltered spot in a Zone 7 garden for a daphne. *Daphne bholua* 'Jacqueline Postill' is exceptional, and *D. odora aureomarginata* is remarkably hardy given a little shelter. It is also worth searching out *D. jezoensis*, an unusual yellow-flowered deciduous daphne which bears its scented flowers in early winter and loses its leaves in summer. Daphnes have a tendency to sulk if planted in containers and do best in the border.

A frost-kissed fir (left) is nature's own decoration during winter. Inside, rings of dried cranberries, bay leaves tied with raffia, scented pine cones and gilded oranges make beautiful Christmas decorations.

On a cold, bright winter's day a foray into the garden provided me with branches of flowering cornelian cherry, and fragrant witch hazel and rosemary, to complement the double-flowered narcissus bought from the florist (right). Planted in a glass bowl (far right), these Soleil d'Or fill the house with their fragrance.

Other recommended fragrant shrubs for Zones 6 or 7 are the winter-flowering viburnum, in particular *Viburnum × bodnantense* 'Dawn', the evergreen Christmas box (*Sarcococca hookerana* var. *digyna* or *S. ruscifolia* var. *chinensis*), and the winter honeysuckle (*Lonicera × purpusii* 'Winter Beauty' or *L. fragrantissima)*. The mimosa (*Acacia dealbata*) is quite tender but will often survive quite successfully for a number of years before being killed off by a particularly hard winter. As it is a fast-growing tree I consider it worth planting and replacing for the reward of its wonderful fragrant flowers. It makes a successful conservatory plant for areas that experience very hard winters.

Where space is limited, bulbs will provide some delicious scent and color in late winter or early spring. *Iris reticulata* is one of my favorites – its deep blue flowers flashed with bright yellow;

Crocus laevigatus 'Fontanayi' is sweetly scented, as is the snowdrop *Galanthus nivalis* 'W Thompson'.

I like to plant a few extra pots of fragrant winter-flowering bulbs so that when they flower, I can give them to friends. As well as the outdoor varieties, I buy bulbs that have been specially prepared for forcing indoors. These are not difficult to grow, provided you start them off cool and dark, move them into the light when the leaf growth has started and then into the warmth when they are well grown. If you try to short-cut this process, the flowers will either bolt or start flowering while still partially formed. With hyacinths – one of the most heady fragrances of the season – I plant them individually in peat pots and then select those which are at the same stage of growth to pot up together and bring indoors.

When the winter weather remains resolutely cold, there aren't many opportunities to enjoy the fragrance of winter flowers, as they need to be warmed by the sun, even briefly, to release their scent. This is when I pick a few to bring indoors for an informal arrangement. Once inside, even a few sprigs will soon fill the air with their perfume. I like to mix the flowers, so that there is an interesting contrast in shapes and textures and a heady blend of fragrance.

Viburnum or witch hazel provide a twiggy outline that can be filled with winter honeysuckle or rosemary and florists' tulips or early narcissus in toning colors. Don't try for symmetry, just fill a vase or jug with a relaxed mix of flowers which will invite you to enjoy their fragrance.

Soleil d'Or bowl

Of all the forced bulbs, the *Narcissus* 'Soleil d'Or' are the easiest to grow and quickly fill the room with a delicious fragrance. Unlike most bulbs, they do not need to be planted in compost, but can instead be grown in a bowl of stones and water. If a glass bowl is used, the stones and the roots of the bulbs can be seen and become an attractive part of the arrangement. Plant in late September or early October and these bulbs will be ready to give as Christmas presents.

Glass bowl, approximately
10 in (25 cm) diameter
Washed stones
(those sold for aquariums are ideal)
10 'Soleil d'Or' bulbs

Half fill the bowl with stones and arrange the bulbs on top. Pour more stones into the bowl until just the "noses" of the bulbs protrude. Add water to the bowl so that the level is halfway up the stones.

Stand the bowl of bulbs in a cool, dark place and check their progress once every two weeks. When the leaves are 2 in (5 cm) high, move to a cool, light position. Continue to check once every two weeks. When the leaves are 6 in (15 cm) high, the bowl can be brought into the warmth. The flowers will last longer if they are introduced to a warmer room slowly. Once there, it may be necessary to add a little water, but only if the bulbs have used up all the water in the bottom of the bowl.

Winter posy

It is not until you examine a snowdrop or hellebore that you can fully appreciate the delicate beauty of these flowers, and while I generally feel that winter flowers are so precious they should be left in the garden, I grow both of these in sufficient numbers to allow me to pick some for posies. Neither snowdrops nor *Helleborus orientalis* are strongly scented, but if combined with fragrant evergreen foliage and herbs they make a posy that is a visual delight and deliciously aromatic.

In the old-fashioned language of flowers, the snowdrop symbolizes hope, the myrtle love and rosemary remembrance, but be careful who you give the posy to if it contains a hellebore as this is said to signify scandal!

3–4 hellebore flowers
20–30 snowdrops
Sprigs of rosemary, myrtle or Christmas box
Ivy leaves
12 in (30 cm) of ½ in (12 mm) wide
white satin ribbon

Use the hellebores for the center of the posy and arrange the sprigs of rosemary, myrtle or box around the flower. Encircle the foliage with snowdrops and finish the posy with a circle of overlapping ivy leaves. Bind with twine and finish with a white satin bow.

If you are taking the posy to a friend, keep it fresh by wrapping the stem ends in wet cotton balls and plastic wrap or foil.

The delicate beauty and soft fragrance of winter flowers and foliage can go unnoticed in the garden. Bound into a posy, their transient beauty is revealed and they become a very special gift.

SPICES come into their own at this time of year. Unlike dried herbs, which need to be replaced every few months, spices will last for a very long while if they are kept upright in airtight jars in a dry, dark store cupboard.

Winter is not a season for frugality, this is a time of hearty meals, warming and nourishing against the cold and wet, of celebratory feasts and occasional over-indulgence. The rich flavors and heady aromas of this time of year are given their intensity by the liberal use of fragrant spices and herbs which we use in much the same way today, as did our forebears over hundreds of years. Mince pies, spice cookies, marzipans, gingerbreads and honey cakes would have been as familiar to the 17th century housewife as they are to us. The spices of the East and West Indies dominate, allspice and ginger from the West Indies and nutmeg, cinnamon and cloves from the East.

When the celebrations are over this is the time of year when we often feel our lowest, when we fall ill and need to be cosseted; when herbs such as sage and chamomile can bring comfort and relief.

Our Christmas pudding was made in November,
All they put in it, I quite well remember:
Currants and raisins, and sugar and spice,
Orange peel, lemon peel – everything nice.

PUDDING CHARMS
Charlotte Druit Cole

ALLSPICE is an evergreen of the myrtle family and gained its name because it is said to taste of a combination of cloves, juniper, cinnamon and pepper. In France it is similarly known as *quatre épices*. It is indigenous to the West Indies, hence its earlier name of Jamaica Pepper, and is also grown in Central and South America. It is unusual among spices as its berries are harvested before they have ripened; if left to ripen on the tree, they lose their aroma and volatile oils.

NUTMEG (Torreya) and *MACE* grow on a vast evergreen tropical tree that can reach 60 ft (20 m) high. The spices are encased in a peach-like fruit which splits open as it ripens to reveal the brilliant scarlet mace, which fades to its characteristic pale gold color when dried. It is not an easy tree to cultivate except where conditions exactly meet its requirements and even then it does not bear fruit for the first nine years and then not in any commercial quantity. Although modern methods are resolving some of these problems, it is understandable that nutmeg plantations were jealously guarded.

The nutmeg is a native of the Moluccas or Spice Islands, which were controlled by the Dutch East India Company from 1602 to 1796. They totally monopolized the trade in this spice, to the extent of actually destroying three-quarters of the nutmeg trees because they grew on small islands that could not be adequately guarded. A French planter eventually succeeded in smuggling out some nutmeg seedlings and establishing them on the equally suitable island of Mauritius. Nowadays there are two major producers of nutmeg, Indonesia and the West Indian island of Grenada.

Nutmeg was extremely fashionable in the 17th and 18th centuries and was used in huge quantities. Although Holland controlled the trade, it was used throughout Europe and in the Middle East.

In England, a pocket nutmeg grater was considered to be an essential accessory in fashionable circles and jewellers were commissioned to make elaborately chased silver versions which the traveller could use for food, wine and possets. Decorative nutmeg boxes were given as wedding presents and housekeepers kept lockable, lacquered spice boxes with several compartments and a central tube which held a circular grater and a couple of nutmegs.

Most traditional Christmas recipes for cakes and cookies seem to contain nutmeg, and although in modern times we have tempered the amount we use, it is still an essential ingredient in festive baking. In Germany, the Christmas cookie, the *Lebkuchen*, had its earliest origins in the cakes baked in the monasteries using honey from the "Honeycomb of the Holy Roman Empire" as the Lorenz Forest was known. The city of Nuremberg was founded nearby and when the trade route to Venice opened in the 14th century, spices, nuts and fruit were added to the recipe. The city is famous for these cookies which have been sold ever since at the Nuremberg Christmas Market. Recipes are jealously guarded, with each baker claiming that their cookie is the authentic *Lebkuchen*.

These beautiful old spice boxes were kept under lock and key by the mistress of the house or the housekeeper and the precious spices were only used under her supervision.

Spiced honey cake

Allspice is one of the spices traditionally used to flavor the delicious honey cake that is made in many European countries. Theoretically, this cake keeps very well, but it never gets the opportunity in our house.

This is an excellent cake to take to a post-Christmas get-together. Wrap it in clear plastic and a new tea-towel tied with a ribbon. Then you can volunteer to help with washing the dishes!

1 stick (110 g) unsalted butter

1½ cups (250 g) soft brown sugar

2 large eggs

2 cups (230 g) self-raising flour

1 tbsp ground almonds

½ tsp ground cinnamon

½ tsp ground cloves

2 tsp ground ginger

Juice and zest of a Seville orange

½–⅔ cup (170–200 ml) milk

2 tbsp honey

Cream the butter and sugar. Beat the eggs and gradually incorporate into the creamed mixture.

Sift the dry ingredients into a bowl and stir in the milk, honey, and orange juice. Carefully fold the flour mixture into the creamed butter/sugar/eggs. Bake in a lined 1 lb (500 g) loaf tin at 350°F/180°C for 1 hour.

CLOVES have similar origins to those of nutmeg. As a native of the Moluccas, the trade in this spice was monopolized by the Dutch for centuries. In Europe, it was much used in potpourris and sweet powders, both for its fragrance and its reputed powers to ward off the plague. The clove is actually the immature flower bud which is harvested and dried early to retain the maximum aroma.

It is traditionally used as a flavoring in apple pies and is an essential spice for Christmas puddings, mincemeat and mulled wine.

In aromatherapy, clove oil is a powerful antiseptic, analgesic and anti-bacterial. It is a traditional cure for toothache and also aids the digestion. It should not be used on the skin unless well diluted as it is an irritant.

This richly spiced cake is the perfect winter tea-time treat. It keeps well, so make a batch to give to friends or to please the family.

Mulling spices

Mulled wine is a gloriously warming drink, perfect for parties and gatherings during the dark winter evenings. It is simply made by pouring two bottles of red wine into a saucepan, together with 4 oz (100 g) sugar, 4 tablespoons of water and a bundle of mulling spices. Heat gently until the sugar has dissolved and serve hot.

For a really seasonal gift, look for a small basket in which to pack two bottles of red wine with mulling spices and instructions. A ready-to-use gift for a pre-Christmas party.

1 orange, washed

1 lemon, washed

Skewer

16 whole cloves

1 tsp powdered cloves

1 tsp powdered cinnamon

1 tsp powdered allspice

1 tsp freshly grated nutmeg

4 muslin squares, 4 × 4 in (10 × 10 cm)

String

8 long cinnamon sticks (or 16 short)

Makes 4 bundles

Remove the peel from the orange and lemon, cut into strips. Use a skewer to make a hole at one end of each strip of peel. Leave the peel in a warm place for one or two days to dry.

Mix the whole cloves and ground spices and place 1 teaspoon in the muslin squares. Gather up and tie with a piece of string.

Tie two large (or four small) cinnamon sticks firmly together with a 8 in (20 cm) length of string. Thread a strip of lemon peel and three of orange peel on to the string, attach a muslin bundle and finish with a bow.

Package as described for a seasonal gift or store in a glass jar ready for use.

The fragrance of mulled wine is a sure sign that the festive season is upon us. Attractively packaged, they will make a classic Christmas gift.

Christmas cookies

The traditional *Lebkuchen* is a substantial softish cookie – this recipe, which can be used for tree decorations, is a lighter version and has a crisper texture. If you wish to retain the traditional softness of the *Lebkuchen* you should store the cookies in a tin with half an apple which will provide sufficient moisture to keep the cookies soft.

3 tbsp (40 g) dark honey

3 tbsp (40 g) soft dark brown sugar

Pinch of fresh ground nutmeg

Pinch of cinnamon

Pinch of ginger

Pinch of cloves

1 tsp brandy

4 tbsp (50 g) butter

Pinch of baking soda

Pinch of baking powder

1 cup (100 g) unbleached all-purpose flour

Confectioner's sugar

Milk

Makes 8–10 cookies

Preheat the oven to 350°F/180°C. Melt the honey and the brown sugar in a pan. Bring to the boil and then remove from heat. Add the spices, brandy, butter, baking soda and baking powder and stir until the butter has melted and the mixture is clear and smooth.

Sift the flour into a bowl and pour in the honey mixture, folding it in to form a soft dough. Roll the dough out on a floured surface to a thickness of ¼ in (6 mm). Cut out using pastry cutters of your own choice.

Make a hole at the top of each cookie through which to thread a ribbon. Bake on a buttered baking sheet for 10 minutes until the cookies are golden brown. When cool, you may frost with a thin confectioner's sugar and milk icing.

These spiced Christmas cookies are traditionally heart-shaped, but taste just as good whatever shape you make them. Thread with ribbon and hang on your tree.

CHAMOMILE *(Anthemis nobilis)* is unusual among the healing herbs in being as popular a remedy today as it has been for many centuries. My bedtime mug of chamomile tea is such an ingrained habit that I actually take my own supply of tea bags with me when I am away from home. Its soothing and digestive properties make it the ideal drink for last thing at night, and although initially an acquired taste, once gained it is a boon and a delight. There are two types of chamomile in common usage both of which have similar properties, the Roman or lawn chamomile *(Anthemis nobilis)* and the German chamomile *(Matricaria chamomilla).*

Chamomile has been in cultivation for thousands of years. In Egypt, it was so revered that it was dedicated to their gods; the Greeks, observing its apple-like scent, named it the "ground apple"; and the Spanish adopted a similar name, *manzanilla*, "a little apple." Chamomile was grown in monastic gardens during the Middle Ages and was known as the "Plants' Physician," as it was said to promote the health of plants growing around it. It was initially found to be relatively difficult to establish so it remained quite rare. However, as its use spread, its aromatic qualities made it a popular strewing herb and lawns were sown with chamomile plants which released their fragrance as you walked upon them. A verse of the time records, "Like a chamomile bed/The more it is trodden/ The more it will spread."

Should you be tempted to establish your own chamomile lawn, there is a flowerless variety, 'Treneague', which is especially suitable for this purpose. You should bear in mind though, that while the end product will be aromatic, it will be more like the medieval idea of a short meadow than a velvety sward.

In homeopathy, chamomile teething granules are a popular remedy for teething babies. Chamomile essential oil is calming and soothing to the digestion, although it should not be used in the early months of pregnancy. Blended with lavender it is an effective cure for insomnia. Use two drops of each in a bath just before bedtime.

Because this plant is so beneficial and gentle in its effect it can be safely used in the home as a mildly sedative drink (when making a tisane, the cup or mug should be covered while it infuses or much of the medicinal effect will be lost in evaporation), as a soothing and healing infusion for the skin, an excellent reviver for tired and irritated eyes and as a hair rinse for blondes. For a concentrated and effective treatment for tired eyes you might like to make some chamomile eye pads (instructions on page 112).

– the season of sudden unexpected fragrances: viburnum, witch hazel and wintersweet, warmed by a wintry sun, of the miraculous appearance of delicately beautiful hellebores, snowdrops and aconites surviving the harshest weather and heralding the lengthening days.

Chamomile eye pads

The easiest way to explain the method of making these eye pads is to draw a comparison with making ravioli – instead of two sheets of pasta, there are two pieces of muslin with a filling of chamomile.

To use, cut two individual eyepads from a strip of muslin and place in a saucer. Pour on 1 tablespoon of boiling water. Cover with another saucer and leave to infuse until cool. Gently squeeze and apply to the eyelids for 15 minutes.

Make these as a novel gift for anyone who is involved in a lot of close work. Fold the bags concertina-wise and tie with yellow ribbons. Arrange in a basket with instructions.

Ruler and pencil

4 oz (100 g) chamomile flowers

2 pieces of muslin each 10 × 10 in (25 × 25 cm)

Pins

Sewing thread

Sewing machine or needle

Basket, ribbons, optional

Makes 16 eyepads

Use a ruler and pencil to mark off 2 in (5 cm) squares on both pieces of muslin, with ⅜ in (1 cm) seam allowances around each square. Place one piece of muslin on a flat surface and put 1 teaspoon of chamomile flowers in the center of each square. Cover with the other piece of muslin and pin. Sew along the guidelines. Cut four strips of eyepads, being careful to cut between the seam allowances.

SAGE (*Salvia officinalis*) is native to the Mediterranean and Syria, but has been cultivated throughout Europe for many centuries. The botanical name is derived from the Latin *salveo* 'I am well', and indicates its importance as a healing herb. For thousands of years, its curative properties have been valued, and women weakened by, plague were plied with sage tea to restore their health and increase their fertility. In medieval times, sage was a key herb in the infirmary garden of monasteries and the herb was used to treat a wide range of illnesses. In the 18th century, the herbalist John Hill said of this herb, "Sage will

Tired, irritated eyes will regain some of their sparkle when treated with chamomile eye pads. A thoughtful and appropriate gift for a workaholic or a busy mother, especially when you provide her with the time to enjoy the treatment.

Sage and honey tea

retard that rapid progress of decay that treads upon our heels so fast in the latter years of life, will preserve the faculties and memory, more valuable to the rational mind than life itself without them." This belief was not confined to Britain; throughout Europe and the Middle East, scholars and doctors wrote of the life-enhancing qualities of the sage. Eventually, its reputation reached China where it became so prized that the Dutch merchants were able to indulge in a highly profitable trade of exchanging one sack of sage leaves for three sacks of the finest quality China tea.

There are many species of sage that grow in other parts of the world and have found use in traditional medicines. Native Americans mixed ground sage leaves with bear fat to make a healing salve and use burning bundles of dried sage as a type of incense for ritual purification.

The most popular way to take sage has always been in a tisane or tea and whether you are using it regularly to "quicken the senses and the memory" or as a soothing winter drink for a sore throat, it makes a delicious hot beverage somewhat reminiscent of chamomile tea. The red sage has always been the favored variety for medicinal use, although I also find that the golden sage *Salvia officinalis* 'Icterina' makes a delicious and attractive tisane. Crumbled dried sage can be used (1 teaspoon per 1 pint [600 ml]) but I prefer the taste and appearance of fresh sage and keep my red sage plant *S. officinalis purpurea* under a cloche during the winter months to guarantee a supply of leaves.

A basket containing a tisane glass with a jar of honey and a sage plant makes a nice gift for a health-conscious friend or someone confined to bed with a cold. Copy out the following recipe and tuck it into the basket.

1 oz (25 g) torn sage leaves
2 tbsp honey
Juice of 1 lemon
2½ cups (600 ml) boiling water
Serves 4 glasses of tea

Place the sage, honey and lemon juice in a jug. Pour on the boiling water, stir until the honey has dissolved and leave to infuse for 30 minutes.

Winter colds and sore throats can be a trial for the invalid and for the person left to nurse the patient. Take five minutes to sit down and share a pot of soothingly delicious sage and honey tea. It will do you both good and show you care.

Winter potpourri

This potpourri is a rich blend of fragrant oils and spices mixed with fir cones, orange peel, cranberries and pine to create a mixture that both complements and echoes the fragrances of the festive season. I have found the most successful way to dry cranberries is to thread them on wire and hang them up in a warm place. This way they keep a good strong color and are dry within a week.

I have used a fairly complex blend of oils which is well worth the trouble if you are making a large batch of potpourri. For smaller quantities, you can create a simpler blend by combining four parts mandarin oil to one part cedarwood and one part cinnamon. Do use rubber gloves when mixing the spices and oils if you have sensitive skin.

Potpourri is also a welcome gift. Pack some into clear bags tied with tartan ribbon to give as aromatic Christmas gifts.

When making this potpourri, I blend a double quantity of the oil and after Christmas I add this to the potpourri before packing it away in a tightly sealed tin for use next year.

POWDERED SPICE BLEND
1 tbsp fresh ground nutmeg
1 tbsp powdered cinnamon
1 tbsp powdered cloves
¾ oz (15 g) gum benzoin

OIL BLEND
1 tsp (5 ml) mandarin essential oil

80 drops (4 ml) cedarwood essential oil
60 drops (3 ml) cinnamon essential oil
40 drops (2 ml) clove essential oil
20 drops (1 ml) frankincense essential oil

WHOLE SPICE BLEND
2 oz (40 g) star anise
½ oz (10 g) juniper berries
¾ oz (15 g) cloves
8 cinnamon sticks, broken into large pieces
1 oz (25 g) shredded oakmoss

BASIC MIX
1 lb (500 g) mixed cones
Sprigs of pine
Dried peel of 4 oranges
4 oz (100 g) dried cranberries

Lidded bowl or large bag
Makes large bowl of potpourri

Luxuriously aromatic winter potpourri is redolent with seasonal fragrances of cinnamon, mandarin, frankincense and cloves and is crammed with wonderful cones, barks and peels to make a mixture that looks as good as it smells. For a truly magnificent gift, make up brocade bags to fill with potpourri.

Place the powdered spices in a small glass or china mixing bowl. Add the oil blend to the spices, mixing it well; it should make a damp, crumbly mixture. Add the whole spices and cinnamon sticks. Shred the oakmoss and add it to the mixture.

Place the mixture in a large lidded earthenware bowl or a bag. Add the cones, sprigs, orange peel and berries. Mix well and seal. Leave to cure for up to six weeks, shaking or stirring occasionally.

Oranges and bay

Dried oranges are being used increasingly as attractive aromatic decorations. They are simple to dry at home, and when threaded together with bay leaves and cinnamon sticks, they make an unusual decorative swag. Use fresh bay leaves, because the dry leaves are quite brittle and tend to break as you thread them on to the string.

Dry the oranges when you have finished cooking by putting them in the cooling oven. As they dry, the flesh will shrink and each orange will segment.

To make a really aromatic gift, scent each dried orange with 2 drops of sweet orange oil and one of cinnamon.

3 oranges
Skewers
Roasting tin
1 yd (1 m) coarse garden string
8 cinnamon sticks
100 fresh bay leaves
1 large darning needle
Makes a swag 30 in (75 cm) long

To dry the oranges, make a series of vertical cuts through the skin and into the flesh of each orange. Thread 3 or 4 oranges on to skewers, making sure the skewer enters and exits the orange through the slits. Rest the skewers across a roasting tin so that the oranges are suspended without touching the tin. Stand the roasting tin in a cooling oven until the skins have hardened. Once this initial drying has taken place, the oranges can be removed to a warm place to complete the drying process.

Once the oranges are dry, you are ready to make the swag. Tie a knotted loop at one end of the string. Tie a cinnamon stick on to the string

This simple, natural swag is a refreshing change to the glitter and tinsel of many Christmas garlands.

ORANGES (Citrus) originated in China and South-East Asia. The bitter orange (*Citrus auranatium*) first arrived in the Mediterranean in the first and second centuries, but it was the Arabs who really established its popularity when they brought the fruit to Spain around the 6th century. The bitter or Seville orange remained paramount until the introduction of the sweet orange (*C. sinensis*) during the 17th century, and even then the bitter orange remained the favorite for cooking and provided its fine essential oils to be used in perfumes, colognes and pots pourris.

Orange trees were highly fashionable and their growing was espoused by royalty and the nobility. No banquet was complete without a serving of oranges in some form or other. The Medici family incorporated five golden oranges into their coat of arms; magnificent orangeries were built at grand houses and Wimbledon became the home of an "Orange Court" of 60 trees. Columbus took oranges to the West Indies, while the Spaniards introduced them to Florida and later California.

The sweet orange first came to Europe via Portugal in the 17th century from where it rapidly spread throughout Europe. Today, the sweet orange reigns supreme, while the Seville orange is only available for a brief six weeks of the year, very different from the 17th century when the first fruit arrived in England at Allhallowstide (1 November) and continued to be available until the end of April or later. Whenever possible, use Seville oranges in cooking, preserves, for drying and pomanders.

next to the loop, then thread 10 bay leaves on to the string using the darning needle. Attach another cinnamon stick and a further 10 bay leaves, before threading on the first orange.

Repeat this process, alternating cinnamon sticks, bay leaves and oranges, until you have used them all, then tie a loop at the other end.

Gilded oranges

Once I had mastered drying oranges, I decided to experiment with various finishes and was very excited with the results I obtained when I gilded oranges using metal leaf. Metal leaf, also known as Dutch metal, is a cheaper alternative to gold leaf and is sold in small sheets with a paper backing.

For the "distressed Venetian look," which leaves some of the orange skin still showing, I use only metal leaf, while for the "dazzling Rococo finish," I add gilt powder to ensure that the entire fruit is gilded.

Decorated with a filmy gauze bow these gilded oranges make stunning aromatic tree decorations and unusual Christmas gifts.

Dried oranges
Water-based gilding size
(this makes the metal leaf stick)
Small paintbrush
Metal leaf, 1 leaf per orange
Scissors
Soft mop-head brush
Gilt powder, gold in color
Gift packaging, optional

Paint half the orange with size. Leave until tacky, about 3–5 minutes. In the meantime, cut pieces of metal leaf (with the backing) to approximately the same size as the orange segments. Apply the leaf, metal side down to each segment, rubbing the paper-backing firmly to ensure that the leaf adheres to the orange.

Peel off the paper and brush gently with the mop-head brush. This will mold the leaf to the orange so that the texture of the skin shows through. Repeat the same process on the other half of the orange.

For a "Venetian" finish, set the orange aside for two hours and then polish vigorously with a soft cloth. For a "Rococo" finish, dust any visible part of the orange and then set aside for two hours before burnishing.

These gilded dried oranges are a natural alternative to the usual Christmas baubles. The oranges are gilded using metal leaf, which is an inexpensive alternative to gold leaf, and are burnished to give a glowing finish.

Orange wine

This fortified wine is traditionally drunk in France at Christmas and New Year. When my children were small we had a French au pair living with us whose mother would send me a bottle of this delicious home-made aperitif to toast *Réveillon* (Christmas Eve). It needs to be made two months before Christmas, but will keep for three or four years.

Apart from being good for fortifying adult carol singers when they call at your door, orange wine makes a lovely and unusual Christmas gift.

5 oranges, washed and quartered

1 sliced lemon

1 vanilla pod

½ teaspoon freshly grated nutmeg

2 bottles (1.5 litres) of red Côtes du Rhône

Muslin

Granulated sugar

½ pint (300 ml) pure *Eau de Vie* or *marc*

Glass demijohn with cork or similar glass container (4 pint / 2.25 litres capacity)

Bottles, corks, labels, etc

Makes approximately 4 bottles

Place oranges, sliced lemon, vanilla pod and nutmeg in the glass container. Pour on the wine, cork tightly and leave for 40 days. Filter the wine through muslin and measure. For every 1¾ pints (1 litre) add ½ cup (100g) sugar. Return to the glass jar, add the *eau de vie/marc*, seal tightly and leave to mature for at least 1 month. Bottle and label.

A traditional French drink for the festive season, orange wine is actually a red wine that has been fortified with spirits and flavored with oranges, spices and sugar. Decoratively packaged, it is an ideal Christmas present.

Orange mincemeat

There was a time when the ready-made mincemeat available in the shops was a very poor substitute for the home-made variety. These days "luxury" mincemeats are much closer to the real thing, but if you have time, it is most satisfying to make some of your own. I have used this recipe for many years and have found none better.

If possible, buy your candied peel in large pieces and cut it up at home, it is generally of far better quality than the ready-chopped variety. Better still, when Seville oranges are in season, candy a large batch for this and other Christmastide recipes. This is a moist mincemeat which will keep well for a year.

Your children's teacher will undoubtedly appreciate a jar of this delicious mincemeat as an alternative to the usual Christmas gift of bath salts or pot plants.

4 oz (100 g) candied orange and lemon peel
1 lb (500g) peeled, cored and chopped apples
8 oz (225g) shredded suet
1⅓ cups (225 g) raisins
1⅓ cups (225 g) sultanas
1⅓ cups (225 g) currants
1½ cups (250g) dark brown sugar
Half a nutmeg, grated
1 cup (100 g) blanched and coarsely chopped almonds
Grated rind and juice of 1 large orange
2 tbsp brandy
3–4 tbsp orange liqueur
Clean, dry jars
Makes approximately 8 jars of mincemeat

Combine the ingredients in the order given above. Mix well and pot and seal in the jars.

Even those suffering 'mince pie fatigue' will find their spirits lifted and their taste buds revitalized by this delicious-tasting and beautifully packaged orange mincemeat. Home-dried orange rings and gilded bay leaves are used to decorate the jars.

ORANGE OILS are extracted from different species of citrus trees. Neroli is extracted from the flowers of the bitter orange (C. *auranatium*) and petitgrain from its twigs and branches. A relative of the bitter orange, C. *bergamia*, is the source of bergamot oil, and orange oil is extracted from the sweet orange (C. *sinensis*). All citrus oils have an uplifting effect. Neroli is particularly useful in treating anxiety and depression, petitgrain is a good oil to use in massage blends and bergamot is wonderfully energizing when added to a bath. Sweet orange is a digestive aid.

If we did not know the orange – if somebody were suddenly to spring upon us a blossom of exquisite ivory color and wonderful perfume, which presently developed into a golden globe, whose very rind was odorous, whose hue was a glory – with what rapture we should receive it.

May Byron

POMANDERS generally conjure up an image of an orange stuck with cloves. The word pomander is derived from the French *pomme d'ambre* and refers to the original apple-shaped lumps of ambergris which were carried in Renaissance Venice. As time passed, the name came to refer to the elaborate filigree containers made of silver, gold, ivory and crystal which were fashioned for the ambergris and other perfumed gums and resins.

In Elizabethan England, the nobility carried pomanders to ward off the stench and pestilence. Queen Elizabeth I always carried one, and the silver pomander belonging to Mary Queen of Scots can still be seen in Edinburgh.

Seville oranges are studded with cloves and then 'cured' in an aromatic spice mixture. This ages-old traditional method has yet to be bettered.

Orange and clove pomanders

The simple orange and clove pomanders are cured in a mixture of spices and fixative and will stay richly fragrant for many months. As the fruit dries and hardens it will shrink, but the pomanders should not be discarded even if the scent fades. Simply dip them briefly in warm water and place them in some curing spice for 4 weeks, turning them regularly, and you will find the fragrance restored. The curing spice will last for at least a year if kept well covered and can be used to make several batches of pomanders.

When studding the orange with cloves, keep them fairly close together, but with sufficient room to allow for shrinkage.

Wrap the pomander in muslin and then two or three layers of gold and silver net, tie with a gold ribbon and bells and hang them on your tree to scent the room and to be given to guests as they depart.

4 oz (100 g) powdered cinnamon

2 oz (50 g) powdered cloves

½ oz (15 g) powdered allspice

½ oz (15 g) powdered nutmeg

1 oz (25 g) orris root powder

Large pottery bowl

Thick darning needle or thin knitting needle

6 unblemished thin-skinned oranges

4 oz (100 g) best quality whole cloves

Plastic wrap

Gift packaging, optional

Mix all the spices and the orris root in the bowl.

Pierce a line of holes around half an orange and stud with cloves. Repeat this process until the whole orange is covered.

Place the orange in the bowl of spices, tossing gently so that the whole surface has come into contact with the spices. Repeat this process for the other oranges. Cover the bowl tightly with plastic wrap.

Turn the pomanders daily (or as often as you remember) for one month. They will then be ready to remove from the spices and use.

Studded all over with spicy cloves, these orange pomanders are packed into festive-colored tissue paper and a pretty box.

Scented pine cones

I love the look of fir cones piled high in a wooden bowl and when their fragrance is enhanced by the addition of essential oils, they become an eye-catching aromatic feature.

Create a wonderful winter gift by lining a wooden box with red felt and filling it with scented pine cones. The felt will absorb the fragrance and provide a colorful background to the pine cones.

20 drops of pine or cedarwood oil
Large glazed china mixing bowl of pine cones
Plastic wrap
Gift packaging, optional

Add the pine or cedarwood oil to the pine cones, turning the cones as you do so to ensure that the oil is well dispersed. Cover the mixing bowl tightly with plastic wrap and leave to stand for 1 week to allow the oils to penetrate the cones.

Place the cones in a decorative container. The oil will slowly evaporate into the room, scenting the air as it does so. Once the scent has faded the cones can be revived by repeating the process above.

If you have an open fire, you can throw a cone or two in occasionally for an intense burst of fragrance.

Pine cones readily absorb fragrant oils which will enhance their already attractive aroma. Simply piled in a bowl they are attractive to look at and will scent the room. Packed in a box they make an original aromatic gift.

Lavender body lotion

Lemon and lavender are both beneficial oils for use in a body lotion as they promote healing, tone and balance, as well as conditioning the skin. The fresh fragrance makes this blend ideal for use by men and women, perfect to use after a workout at the gym or to re-moisturize the skin after a swim.

1 cup (250 ml) of unfragranced moisturizer
30 drops lemon essential oil
30 drops lavender essential oil

Decant the lotion into a china bowl, add the essential oils and stir well before returning the lotion to its bottle. Use within three months.

Give yourself or a friend a winter treat with a gift package of specially blended face oil (right) and a moisturizing body lotion (left).

Gentle face oil

Winter faces sometimes need more attention than the usual moisturizer. A blend of gentle essential oils with sweet almond and wheatgerm oil is the perfect treatment for dry skin. Apply it to damp skin, leave for 10 minutes and then blot off excess with a tissue.

Make up a gift box with a bottle of gentle face oil and a bottle of lavender body lotion as a winter beauty kit. Make some decorative labels giving ingredients and instructions for use.

1 tsp wheatgerm oil
¼ cup (50 ml) sweet almond oil
8 drops rose essential oil
4 drops geranium essential oil
Gift packaging, optional

Add the wheatgerm oil to the almond oil and then add the essential oils. Shake gently to blend. Store in an opaque glass bottle out of direct light and use within one month.

Bibliography

Aromatherapy – a practical guide to essential oils and aromassage by Jan Balkham, Blitz Editions (1994)

At Home with Herbs by Jane Newdick, Storey Publishing, Pownal, Vermont

Essential Oils by Colleen Dodt, Storey Publishing, Pownal, Vermont

Fragrance by Edwin Morris, Charles Scribner's Sons, New York

The Fragrant Pharmacy by Valerie Ann Worwood, Bantam Books – Macmillan, London (1994)

The Herbal Body Book by Stephanie Tourles, Storey Publishing, Pownal, Vermont

Herbal Treasures by Phyllis Shaudys, Garden Way Publishing, Pownal, Vermont

Medieval English Gardens by Teresa McLean, Barrie & Jenkins, London (1989)

A Modern Herbal by Mrs. M. Grieve, Jonathan Cape (1974)

A Natural History of the Senses by Diane Ackerman, Random House, New York

Perfume by Patrick Suskind

Scent in your Garden by Stephen Lacey, Frances Lincoln, London (1991)

The Scented Room by Barbara Ohrbach, Sidgwick and Jackson (1986)

Scents and Sensuality by Max Lake, John Murray (1989)

Sloe Gin and Beeswax by Jane Newdick, Letts, an imprint of New Holland Publishers (1993)

Index

A

Acacia dealbata, see mimosa
After–sun cream 69
Alchemilla mollis 46
Allium sativum, see garlic
Allium schoenoprasum, see chives
allspice 106, 108
All To Sweetness Turns 71
anemone, Japanese 72
Anthemis nobilis, see chamomile
Anethum graveolens, see dill
angelica 8
apple cake 82–83
aquilegia 18–19
aromatherapy 11, 31, 36, 50, 54, 60, 66
Aromatic lavender 88
attar of roses 52, 53, 54
Autumn treat 86–87

B

Bacon, Francis 28
basil 60–62
    essential oil 60
    sauce 61
bath bags 39
bathing 8
bay 62, 100, 116–117
beeswax 40, 91
Beeswax polish 40–41
bellis daisy 18–19
bergamot 45
bergamot essential oil 120
Binyon, Laurence 72
Boules de chèvre 29
Bouquets garnis 62–63
broom 45
Brunfelsia 44
brunnera 18–19
buddleia 45
Burning of the Leaves, The 72
Byron, May 120

C

Calendula officinalis, see marigold
candles, scented 89–91
    beeswax 91

floating 89
Capsicum 64, 78
    C. frutescens 78
    C. minimum 78
chamomile 69, 111, 112
    essential oil 111
Chamomile eye pads 112
Chanel 11, 52, 58
cherry, cornelian 102
chilli 78, 80
Chinese 8
chives 14, 28
Christmas cookies 110
Christmas box 102
chrysanthemum 72, 73, 86–87
Cinnamomum zeylanicum, see cinnamon
cinnamon 81–82
    essential oil 82
Citrus 34, 117
    C. auranatium 117, 120
    C. bergamia 120
    C. sinensis 117, 120
    see also lemon, orange
Citrus potpourri 36–37
citrus trees 34, 45
cloves 108, 122
    essential oil 109
Coeur à la crème 32–33
Concerning Odours 8
conditioning flowers 46
Confit of garlic 79
Convallaria majalis, see lily of the valley
Cosmos atrosanguineus 72
Cowper, William 58
cranberry 100, 114
Crocus laevigatus 'Fontanayi' 102
Culpeper 28, 58

D

Daphne 16, 101
    D. bholua 101
    D. x burkwoodii 'Somerset' 16
    D. jezoensis 101
    D. odora
    D. aureomarginata 101
Datura 45
dill 26

Dioscorides 28
distillation 8, 52, 53, 66
Drayton, Michael 26
Dutch East India Company 9, 106, 108

E

eau de Carmes 8
eau de Cologne 9, 11, 69
Eau de Cologne 94
elder 24
elderflower 24, 25
    cordial 24
    skin tonic 25
Elderflower skin tonic 25
Elizabeth of Hungary 8, 66
enfleurage 8, 58
Epices de Provence 76–77
essential oils 8, 9, 11, 50, 56, 66, 89, 97, 117, 120
    see also aromatherapy
euphorbia 18–19
eye pads 112

F

face oil 125
Floating lights 89
Florida waters 69
Floris, Juan 9
flower waters 11
frankincense 8, 66
freesia 48–49
Fresh tomato and basil sauce 61
Frosted violets 21–22
fuchsia 72
furniture polish 40
Furniture reviver 40–41

G

Galanthus nivalis 102
garlic 78, 79, 80
Gentle face oil 125
Geranium cream 56
geranium, scented 56
Gerard, John 20, 31
Gilded oranges 118
ginger 81
goat cheese 29
grape hyacinths 15, 18–19

Grasse 9, 21, 52, 58
Grieve, Mrs. M. 66, 78
gripe water 28

H

Hamamelis 101
    H. mollis 101
    H. vernalis 'Sandra' 101
Healing herbal ointment 38
Helleborus orientalis 104
herbs 8, 9, 11, 14, 26, 27, 30, 45, 46, 59, 73, 74, 76
    bouquets garnis 62
    drying 76
    pots of 74
    teas 59
    see also sage, thyme, etc
Hill, John 112
Homer 20
honey cake 108
honeysuckle 45, 46
    winter 102
Horace 52, 78
Hungary Water 8, 66
Hurdis, James 16
hyacinth 102

I

incense 8
Iris reticulata 102

J

Japanese 8
jasmine 45, 58
    absolute 11, 58
    Arabian 58
    essential oil 58
    tea 58
Jasminum
    J. angulare 58
    J. officinale 58
    J. sambac 58
    see also jasmine
jelly 84
jonquils 15, 18–19
Joy 11
Joy of Fragrance, The 13
juniper 66, 84
Juniper jelly 84–85
Juniperus, see juniper

L

lady's mantle 46
Land, The 31
Lanvin 11
Lavandula, see lavender
lavender 9, 45, 49, 50, 69, 88
    after-sun cream 69
    essential oil 50
    lotion 125
    sugar 50
    water 9, 50
Lavender body lotion 125
Lavender water 50–51
Lebkuchen 106, 109
lemon 11, 34–37
    essential oil 34, 36
    Meyers 34
    pickling 35
    sugar 35
    trees 34
    vinegar 35
    vodka 35
lemon balm 8, 32
lemon verbena 46, 59, 73
lilac 16, 45
Lilium
    L. candidum 57
    L. regale 57
    see also lily
lily 8, 45, 46, 48–49, 57
    'Casablanca' 57
    roots 57
lily of the valley 15, 16
    scented cologne 16
Lily of the valley pots 17
Lily of the Valley, The 16
lime 59
Lime vinegar 65
Lippia citriodora, see lemon verbena
Lonicera
    L. fragrantissima 102
    L. x purpusii 102
    see also honeysuckle

M

mace 106
Mahonia aquifolium, see oregon grape
maidenhair fern 48
Marie Antoinette 9
marigold, pot 26

marjoram 8, 63, 73
  essential oil 63
massage 8, 56, 97
Massage oils 97
Matricaria chamomilla,
  see chamomile
Melissa officinalis, see
  lemon balm
Menthe
  M. citrata 31
  M. gentilis variegata 31
  M. piperata 31
  M. pulegium 31
  M. requienii 31
  M. rotundifolia
    variegata 31
  M. spicata 31
Meyers lemons 34
Michaelmas daisy 72
mimosa 16, 102
mint 11, 30, 31
  apple mint 31
  Corsican mint 31
  eau de cologne mint 31
  ginger mint 31
  pennyroyal 30
  peppermint 31
  spearmint 31
Molyneux 11
moth repellent 96
moussaka 31
Mulling spices 109
myrrh 8

N
Napoleon 11, 20
narcissus 15, 75, 102,
  103
nasturtium 72
neroli 120
nutmeg 106
Nymphidia 26

O
Ocimum basilicum, see
  basil
oil, culinary 64, 65, 78,
  80
orange 100, 116–123
  essential oil 117, 120
  gilded 100, 118
  pomanders 122–123
  Seville 117, 120, 122

swag 116
Oranges and bay
  116–117
Orange and clove
  pomanders 123
Orange mincemeat 120
Orange wine 119
oregano 63
Origanum, see
  marjoram, oregano
oregon grape 15

P
pansy, winter 75
Parma violet 20
parsley 30
  tea 30
passionflower 45
Patou, Jean 11
Pelargonium
  P. capitatum 56
  P. graveolens 56
  P. odoratissimum 56
  see also geranium
pennyroyal 30
peony 45
perfume 8, 52, 58
petitgrain 120
Petroselinum crispum, see
  parsley
philadelphus 45
phlox 72
Pickled lemons 35–36
pine cones 100, 124
pinks 44, 45
Pizza oil 80
Pliny 20, 52
polyanthus 15
pomades 9
pomanders 54, 122–123
Pompadour, Madame de
  9
posies 18, 46, 104
Pot-et-fleur 48–49
potpourri 9, 14, 50, 56,
  66, 84, 92, 108, 114
  autumn 92
  citrus 36–37
  summer 68
  winter 114
Pots of herbs 74
primrose 15
pumpkin 73, 86–87

Q
Queen Anne's lace 44,
  48–49

R
raita 31
Rhododendron luteum 16
Roasted chili and garlic
  oil 80
Roget & Gallet 11
Rolled beeswax candle
  91
Rosa
  R. centifolia 53
  R. gallica officinalis 53
  see also rose
rose 8, 11, 44, 45, 46,
  52–54, 73
  absolute 54
  apothecary's 53
  attar of 52, 53, 54
  'Belle de Crecy' 53
  breeding 53
  'Constance Spry' 45
  essential oil 52, 53, 54
  'Gloire de Dijon' 45
  'Guinee' 45
  'Louis Odier' 53
  'Madame Isaac
    Pereire' 53
  essential oil 54
  Provence 53
  'Roseraie de L'Hay'
    53
  sugar 52
  -water 52, 53, 54
Rose-berries 99
rosebuds 54
rosehip 73
Rosmarinus officinalis, see
  rosemary
rosemary 14, 66, 73, 102
  essential oil 66
Rosemary hair rinse 67
Rose sugar 53

S
Sackville-West, Vita 16,
  31
saffron 81
sage 8, 59, 73, 112–113
Sage and honey tea 113
Salvia 45, 72

S. discolor 45
S. officinalis, see sage
S. rutilans 45
Sambucus nigra, see elder
sandalwood 8
Sarcococca hookeriana
  102
  S. ruscifolia 102
Scented bath bags 39
Scented flowerpot
  candles 90
scented geranium 56
Scented linen bags 95
Scented pine cones 124
Scented rose ball 54–55
Shakespeare, William 20,
  22, 62
Sissinghurst 16
snowdrop 102, 104
Soleil d'Or bowl 103
southernwood 46, 96
Southernwood moth
  sachets 96
spice 9, 11, 76–78,
  81–83, 104–110
Spiced apple cake
  82–83
Spiced honey cake 108
Spice Trade 9
Spring cordial 24
Spring posy 18
star jasmine 45
sugar, flower 35, 50, 52
Summer posy 46–47
Summer potpourri 68
sweet pea 44, 45, 46
Sweet pepper oil 64

T
tarragon 14, 73
Task, The 58
tea, see tisane
Theophrastus 8
Thomas, Edward 71
thyme 8, 59, 63, 73
  lemon 63, 73
Thymus x citriodorus 63
  T. drucei 63
  T. fragrantissimus 63
  T. herba barona 63
  T. serpyllum 63
  T. vulgaris 63
  see also thyme

tisane 31, 59, 111, 113
Tisanes 59–60
Torreya, see nutmeg
Trachelospermum
  jasminoides 45
tomato and basil sauce 61

V
vetiver 8
Viburnum 15, 102
  V. x bodnantense 102
  V. x burkwoodii 15
  V. x carlesii 16
  V. x juddii 16
vinegar 9, 35, 65
  lemon 35
  lime 65
  mint 65
  tarragon 65
Viola odorata, see violet
Violet salad 22
violet 20, 21, 22
  crystallized 21
  frosting 21
  salad 22
  sugar 21
  syrup of 20
Virgil 20
vodka, lemon 35

W
wallflower 15
walnut oil dressing 22
Walton, Izaak 49
Webb, Mary 13, 99
Wells, Charles Jeremiah
  38
wine 110, 119
Winter pansy trough 75
Winter posy 104–105
Winter potpourri
  114–115
Winter's Tale, A 62
Wisteria venusta 16
witch hazel 101, 102

Y
Yardley, Thomas 9

Z
Zingiber officinale 81